All legislative Powers herein granted shall be vested in a Congress of the United States, which shall consist of a Senate and House of Representatives.

—Constitution of the United States
Article I, Section 1

INTO THE THIRD CENTURY

THE CONGRESS

By

RICHARD B. BERNSTEIN

and

JEROME AGEL

WALKER AND COMPANY
NEW YORK

First published in the United States of America in 1989
by the Walker Publishing Company, Inc.

Published simultaneously in Canada by Thomas Allen & Son
Canada, Limited, Markham, Ontario.

Library of Congress Cataloging-in-Publication Data

Bernstein, Richard B., 1956–
    Into the third century. The congress / by Richard B.
Bernstein and Jerome Agel.
       p. cm.
    Includes index.
    Summary: A history of the United States Congress, ranging
from its foundation in the days of the American Revolution to
the present.
    ISBN 0-8027-6832-6. ISBN 0-8027-6833-4 (lib. bdg.)
    1. United States Congress—History—Juvenile literature.
[1. United States Congress—History.] I. Agel, Jerome.
II. Title. III. Series.
JK1021.B47 1989
328.73'09—dc19   88-21025
                                                  CIP
                                                   AC

Printed in the United States of America

10 9 8 7 6 5 4 3 2 1

Into the Third Century

For my mother, my first teacher, with love.

R.B.B.

The Congress

For Megan Hanford and Daniel Hanford . . . future leaders of the rising generation.

R.B.B.

CONTENTS

INTRODUCTION

The people of the United States govern themselves under a Constitution now two centuries old. It was written in the days of horse-drawn carriages and sailing ships, of powdered wigs and knee-breeches. Its authors, a few dozen men from twelve struggling states along the Atlantic Ocean, had never heard of personal computers or space satellites or nuclear reactors, of airplanes or railroads or automobiles.

The Constitution does not govern this country. "We the People of the United States" do that. We choose the people who will make our laws, enforce them, and settle disputes arising under them. Our Constitution establishes three branches of government: the legislative, the executive, and the judiciary. Each of these three branches has the power to check or restrain the other two branches. The three branches have often worked together and, just as often, they have worked against one another. They are held in a delicate balance by the commands of the Constitution. This system of government has turned out to be strong enough to deal with national problems, flexible enough to adapt to changing times and conditions, and limited enough to avoid damaging our rights.

This is one of three books about the central institutions of our system of government: Congress, the Presidency, and the Supreme Court. Reading all three volumes will introduce you to two centuries of American history, as well as to the history of each institution. You will also learn about the leading figures in each institution's history—the people who have helped to make our system of government work. Some important events appear in only one or two of the three books. This is because our system of government divides power among the three branches of our government. Therefore, some major problems in our history have been the business of only one branch or of two of the three.

INTO THE THIRD CENTURY
THE CONGRESS

CHAPTER ONE

INVENTING A LEGISLATURE

The system of government created in 1787 by the U.S. Constitution has three parts: the legislative branch, or Congress (composed of the House of Representatives and the Senate); the executive branch, directed by the President; and the judicial branch, headed by the Supreme Court.

Every American knows something about the Presidency, and more and more in recent years the Supreme Court has become part of our daily lives. But the Congress remains the unknown branch of our government. And most of the people who do know something about Congress do not see Congress in a flattering light. They are convinced that it is filled with politicians scheming to reward selfish interest groups and to keep themselves in office.

The problem is that most people do not appreciate the importance of the day-to-day grind of politics to the preservation of our liberties and the achievement of important national goals. The history of Congress shows the importance of politics in the development of our government and the nation it is to govern.

This book sketches the history of Congress, from its roots

in the colonial and Revolutionary periods to our own time. It focuses on the place of Congress in our constitutional system. It also describes the three major functions and responsibilities of Congress: to make laws, or *legislate;* to discuss major national issues, or *debate;* and to *investigate* national problems, the workings of government, and the need for new laws.

There is a reason that Congress comes first in the Constitution (in Article I). The delegates to the Federal Convention who drafted the Constitution in 1787 drew on their experience of government during the American Revolution and on their memories of colonial government before the Revolution. In both cases, they were most familiar with legislatures.

Nearly two centuries passed between the establishment of the first permanent English settlement at Jamestown, Virginia, in 1607, and the American declaration of independence from Great Britain in 1776. During that period the colonists relied on their representatives in the colonial legislatures to protect their rights and defend their interests with the mother country. The colonial legislatures had two houses. The lower house was made up of representatives of the people. (In those days, that meant white male property owners, the only people allowed to vote.) The upper house was elected by the lower house, appointed by the Royal governor, or elected by the lower house from candidates named by the governor.

The colonial legislatures modeled themselves on the British Parliament. The colonists thought of themselves as Englishmen with the rights of Englishmen, and their heritage was the history and heritage of Great Britain. Parliament had two houses: the House of Commons, which represented the voters, and the House of Lords, where the nobility took part in government. The American colonists admired the many courageous battles for the rights of Englishmen fought by the House of Commons against the Crown. They also appreciated the important role of the House of Lords as a balance between the Commons and the Crown. This history influenced the leaders of the Revolutionary movement in shaping new governments after the declaration of independence from England.

The American Revolution began as a disagreement between politicians in London and the colonists over how much authority Parliament had to make laws for the colonies—specifically, tax laws. The colonists claimed that under the unwritten English constitution, they could be taxed only by legislatures that they had a direct voice in choosing. The colonists were not represented in Parliament; therefore, Parliament could not impose taxes on them. Parliament replied that although the colonists could not elect anyone to Parliament, they were nevertheless represented because every member of Parliament had the duty to watch over the interests and defend the rights of every subject of the British Empire.

As disputes between the colonists and Great Britain increased, the colonists called meetings of delegates from all the colonies to discuss their common problems with Great Britain and what they should do about them. These meetings were called *congresses*. The Stamp Act Congress met in 1765, the First Continental Congress in 1774, and the Second Continental Congress beginning in May 1775.

It was the Second Continental Congress that took the critical steps leading to the Americans' decision to declare independence from Great Britain. In May 1776, that Congress adopted a resolution written by John Adams of Massachusetts calling on the colonies to adopt new forms of government—that is, to write new state constitutions. On July 2, 1776, that Congress adopted a resolution offered by Richard Henry Lee of Virginia declaring "that these united colonies are, and of right ought to be, free and independent States." And two days later, on July 4, 1776, that Congress adopted the revised and edited Declaration of Independence, drafted by Thomas Jefferson of Virginia.

The Second Continental Congress was also responsible for the first charter of government of the United States of America. That summer and fall, the delegates wrangled over a draft prepared by John Dickinson of Pennsylvania. Not until a year later, in November 1777, did the delegates agree on a final version of this new charter: the Articles of Confederation. All thirteen states had to approve, or *ratify*, the proposed new charter to put it into effect; it was not until March 1781 that the last holdout, Maryland, ratified the Articles.

The Articles of Confederation created only one institution of government: the one-house Confederation Congress. The delegates did not create two houses for this new legislature of the United States because all previous congresses had had only one house. Also, as we shall see, the delegates kept most powers of government in the hands of the states. They did not see any need to establish a traditional form of government with checks and balances or separation of powers at the national level.

The delegates who drafted the Articles of Confederation were suspicious of strong central government, as most Americans were in this period. They believed that government should be placed as close to the people as possible. For these reasons, the government created by the Articles of Confederation was extremely weak.

The one-house Confederation Congress could propose, it could resolve, it could issue requisitions (that is, demands to the states for money and supplies). But it had no power to tax the people directly, no power to regulate trade across state lines, and no power to make the thirteen state governments comply with its requisitions. It could handle foreign affairs and negotiate treaties, such as the Treaty of Paris of 1783 that ended the Revolutionary War, but it could not make the state governments obey the requirements of that treaty. It could issue instructions on relations with the Indians, but it could not prevent the states from cheating, robbing, or waging war on the Indians if they felt like it.

On June 28, 1783, a detachment of soldiers from the Continental Army marched on the Confederation Congress and stuck their muskets through the windows of the building in Philadephia where Congress was meeting. They demanded that Congress make good on the back pay the soldiers were owed. The crisis was resolved, but the delegates were humiliated and never forgot the experience.

Naturally, you might think that so weak a government would be amended, or changed, as soon as people realized that there was a problem. But all thirteen state legislatures had to agree to adopt an amendment, and there was always one or another holdout state to go against the will of the other twelve. By the mid-1780s, the Confederation Congress seemed to be little more than a bad joke.

General George Washington was appalled. He had had to put up with a divided, angry, and confused Congress throughout the long Revolutionary War. As the former Commander-in-Chief of the Continental Army watched anxiously from retirement at his Virginia plantation, Mount Vernon, he realized that the affairs of the United States in peacetime were even more tangled and uncertain than they had been during the war. He exclaimed in one of his many despairing letters during the 1780s: "We are fast verging to anarchy and confusion!"

Other American statesmen were also trading disgusted observations about American politics. One of them was John Jay of New York. The veteran diplomat had been a New York delegate to the Second Continental Congress and President of that body for one year and since the end of 1784 was Secretary for Foreign Affairs to the United States in Congress Assembled—the Confederation Congress. As Secretary, he had tried bravely to keep the United States on the board in the game of power politics, but the Confederation Congress seemed too divided, too distracted, and too weak to back him up. More than practically anyone else in American politics, Jay knew the strengths and weaknesses of the Articles of Confederation. In a letter to George Washington, he suggested that the Articles needed a thorough overhaul, if not a replacement, and he stated the basic principle that such an overhaul should follow: "Let Congress legislate—let others execute—let others judge."

As John Jay, George Washington, James Madison, Alexander Hamilton, and their colleagues were writing back and forth about the problems of the Confederation Congress and the United States, a process was taking shape to promote just such an overhaul.

The first step was the Mount Vernon Conference of 1785, at which Virginians and Marylanders amiably settled problems between the two states, such as navigation on the Potomac River. The Virginians were so pleased with the meeting that they suggested that all the states send delegates to Annapolis, Maryland, in September of 1786 to discuss problems of trade and commerce under the Articles of Confederation.

The Annapolis Convention of 1786 did not fulfill the hopes of its organizers. Only twelve delegates from five states showed up. They were too few to make any serious proposals, but they did electrify the country with their report. Drafted by young, combative Alexander Hamilton, this report declared that the Articles of Confederation were too weak and fragile to work as a plan of government. Hamilton's report urged that a new convention be called to meet in Philadelphia, Pennsylvania, in May 1787 to make the government of the United States adequate to the needs of the Union. Several states responded immediately to this call for action. Others waited for the Confederation Congress to respond before acting.

Finally, on February 21, 1787, the Confederation Congress

did authorize what we now know as the Federal Convention. The delegates voted, however, to give the Convention only the authority to propose amendments to the Articles of Confederation.

On May 25, 1787, the Federal Convention began its work in a stuffy room on the second floor of the Pennsylvania State House—the building we now call Independence Hall. The first action the delegates took was to scrap the Articles and start over, writing a totally new charter of government: the Constitution of the United States.

Most of the Convention's work focused on designing the new legislature of the United States. The delegates decided to keep the name *Congress*. They had to face two more issues: how Congress should be constructed and what powers it should have.

The first issue had to do with *representation*. Who should be represented: the people or the states? Under the old Continental and Confederation Congresses, each state had an equal vote. The delegates from the large states, such as Pennsylvania, wanted each state to have representatives allotted based on population, or wealth, or size, or some other "fair" system. The delegates from the small states, such as Delaware and New Jersey, resisted this idea. They feared that they would be swallowed up by the large states unless they had an equal vote. The fight dragged on all through June and into July. Finally, a compromise proposed by the Connecticut delegates Roger Sherman, William Samuel Johnson, and Oliver Ellsworth was adopted. Their idea is still built into the Constitution today.

Congress has two houses:

1. In the House of Representatives, the people of each state are represented. Each state gets a certain number of representatives based on its population. Its members are elected by the people of each state to serve for two years. The House has the sole power to propose *money bills*—that is, appropriations

and taxation measures. The House elects a presiding officer, called the Speaker of the House (a term borrowed from the British Parliament).

2. The Senate has two Senators from each state, preserving an equal vote for the large and small states. The Senators serve six-year terms. The Senate has the sole power to approve or reject treaties made by the President and to approve or reject the President's nominees for federal judgeships and executive offices. The Senate also works with the House in framing and revising proposals for laws, known as *bills*. The Vice President of the United States presides over the Senate's meetings and has the power to vote to break ties of that body. (The first Vice President, John Adams, holds the record for breaking ties; he did it twenty-nine times.) Under the Constitution of 1787, Senators were chosen by the state legislatures, which were free to authorize popular elections or to choose the Senators themselves. (This system lasted for over a century, until the Seventeenth Amendment, calling for the direct election of Senators, was adopted in 1913.)

Another compromise the delegates adopted set the formula for representation in the House of Representatives: Each state would receive representatives based on the number of free inhabitants plus three-fifths of "all other persons"—a tactful way of saying *slaves*. This compromise was a concession to the Southern slaveholding states. They had threatened to walk out of the Convention if their states were not protected by such a compromise.

There was little fuss about the other issue, the powers of Congress. Congress was given a set of specific powers in Article I, Section 8 of the new charter. These powers amounted to far more than the Confederation Congress ever had. They included the power "to lay and collect Taxes, Duties, Imposts and Excises, to pay the Debts and provide for the common Defence and general Welfare of the United States"; "to regulate Commerce with foreign Nations, and among the several States, and with the Indian Tribes"; "to coin Money" and "to borrow Money on the credit of the United States"; "to establish Post Offices and post Roads"; to issue patents to inventors and copyrights to authors, composers, and artists to protect their rights to their works; "to raise and support Armies" and "to provide and maintain a Navy"; and so forth.

The delegates included a special clause at the end of Article I, Section 8: "To make all Laws which shall be necessary and proper for carrying into Execution the foregoing Powers, and all other Powers vested by this Constitution in the Government of the United States, or in any Department or Officer thereof." This clause has become known as the *elastic clause* because later Congresses and Presidents and the Supreme Court have found in it authority for all sorts of federal statutes, such as the civil rights laws, even though the statutes have no clear authorization in the listed powers of Congress.

The delegates intended Congress to play special roles in checking and balancing the two other branches of government, the Presidency and the Supreme Court. They provided that the President can name certain government officers and negotiate treaties with foreign nations "with the advice and consent of the Senate." They provided that Congress has the power to establish federal courts below the Supreme Court and to define the kinds of cases that the federal courts could hear.

But Congress does not have the power to adopt laws all by itself. Following British precedent and the constitutions of the states of New York and Massachusetts, the Constitution provides that *both* houses of Congress must pass a bill. Any bill passed by the House and Senate then goes to the President. He may sign it into law or return it "with his Objections"—that is, *veto* the bill. A vetoed bill goes back to the chamber that proposed it. If the bill is passed again by at least two-thirds of *both* the House and the Senate, Congress has *overridden* the President's veto, and the bill becomes law. The President may also veto a bill by a more complicated means— if he takes no action on a bill for ten days after getting it, and Congress adjourns before that ten-day period is up, he has carried out a *pocket veto* of the bill.

The Constitution sets forth a special process, known as the *impeachment* process, by which Congress can remove from office "the President, Vice President and all civil Officers of the United States" who have committed "Treason, Bribery, or other high Crimes and Misdemeanors." In this process, the House *impeaches,* or accuses, the official in question, and the Senate conducts a trial of the official on the charges listed in the *articles of impeachment* adopted by the House. A two-thirds vote of the Senate is necessary to convict the official and remove him or her from office.

The delegates to the Federal Convention borrowed the impeachment process from British practice. Also, impeachment had been a favorite tool of the colonial legislatures to keep other government officials in line. Under the Constitution, if the President has been impeached, the Chief Justice of the United States presides over the Senate's trial; if anyone else has been impeached, the Vice President presides over the Senate's trial.

Finally, Congress has the principal responsibility for *amending* the Constitution. Under Article V, there are two ways to make formal changes in the Constitution. The more usual way is for Congress to propose an amendment to the states, by a two-thirds vote of both the House and the Senate. Three-fourths of the states must then ratify the proposed amendment to make it part of the Constitution. There is another way to amend the Constitution, also involving Congress, which has never been used: Two-thirds of the states must apply to Congress to call a special convention to propose amendments to the Constitution. Any amendments proposed by this convention must then be adopted by three-fourths of the states to become part of the Constitution.

On September 17, 1787, thirty-nine of the forty-two delegates to the Convention still present signed the Constitution and sent it by stagecoach to the Confederation Congress, which was sitting in New York City. After several days of argument and debate, Congress sent it on to the states on September 28. The states called special elections to *ratifying conventions*—bodies chosen by the voters for the sole purpose of voting to adopt or to reject the proposed Constitution.

The contending forces in the ratification controversy said and wrote surprisingly little about the proposed new Congress. The opponents of the Constitution—the Anti-Federalists— argued that the new Congress would be too small to ensure that all the people (about four million at that time) would be fairly represented. Some criticized the sweeping grants of power to Congress. Others denounced the compromises with slavery that gave "extra" representation to the slaveholding states. In *The Federalist,* a brilliant series of eighty-five newspaper essays written under the pen name Publius, Alexander Hamilton, James Madison, and John Jay defended the Constitution against these and other charges by the Anti-Federalists.

After ten months of often heated discussion, eleven state ratifying conventions voted to adopt the new Constitution. Unlike the Articles, the Constitution needed ratification by only nine states for it to go into effect. In October 1788, the dying Confederation Congress adopted procedures to help the new charter of government take effect.

CHAPTER TWO

"IN A WILDERNESS WITHOUT A PATH TO GUIDE US"

James Madison of Virginia was one of the most gifted politicians the United States has ever produced. He had served for several years in the Virginia legislature and the Confederation Congress. He had also been a principal delegate to the Federal Convention of 1787 and one of the most important leaders of the successful campaign to win adoption of the Constitution. He spent the fall and winter of 1788 mulling over the next steps that the country—and he—should take.

Madison wanted desperately to be a member of the House of Representatives in the First Congress. He was not pleased to discover that the Virginia legislature, led by the silver-tongued Anti-Federalist orator Patrick Henry, had put Madison's home town of Orange smack in the middle of an Anti-Federal legislative district or that his friend James Monroe, a popular Anti-Federalist, was planning to run against him. Madison and Monroe traveled throughout the district in the winter of 1788–1789, debating the issues before the voters of the region. Madison handily defeated Monroe and thus was ready to return to New York City, the first—temporary—capital of the United States under the Constitution.

When Madison arrived in New York, he discovered that few of his colleagues of either branch of the new First Congress had arrived. He looked over a list of the new Representatives and Senators. As was usual with the short, frail, pessimistic Virginian, gloom overtook him. He wrote to Thomas Jefferson that there were few men in either house of Congress who seemed likely to take on the burden of work that setting up a government would demand. He also wrote that the new Congress would be wandering "in a wilderness without a path to guide us." What Jefferson probably knew as he read the letter, and what actually happened, was that Madison, as usual, shouldered the burden of leading his colleagues in getting the government off the ground.

The Congress was the first branch of the new government to begin its work. It had to count the electoral votes from the states to determine who the first President and Vice President were to be, and it had to write the laws setting up the executive departments and the judicial system. On April 6, 1789, the House and the Senate had the necessary minimum number of members to do business—what legislators call a *quorum*. They met in joint session to count the electoral votes. They were the first Americans to learn officially that George Washington was the unanimous choice to be the first President and that John Adams, with the second greatest number of electoral votes, was elected the first Vice President. After sending messengers to Mount Vernon, Virginia, and to Braintree, Massachusetts, to inform Washington and Adams of the news, Congress got back to work.

The House of Representatives began a small political revolution by permitting anyone, even reporters, to attend its sessions. The Senate continued to meet behind closed doors, as most legislatures at all levels had done in the United States and in Europe. (We get most of what we know about the Senate in this early period from the diary of Senator William Maclay of Pennsylvania, a hard-bitten frontiersman who had

Collections of the Library of Congress

Representative James Madison of Virginia was the leading
member of the House of Representatives during the first four
Congresses (1789–1797). Among his many accomplishments
was his primary role in the framing of the first ten Amendments
to the Constitution, which we call the Bill of Rights.

nothing but scorn for secrecy, pomp, and pretense.) As a
result, the people found the House much more interesting
and had more respect for it.

The House quickly won the interest and favor of the people
because it actually was getting work done. Rumors swept the
capital and the country that the Senators and the Vice
President were wasting their energies arguing about formal
titles for officials of the new government. There was a good
deal of truth to these rumors, and John Adams soon discovered that he was a political laughingstock.

The House took the lead in all but one major piece of
legislation. It deferred to the Senate in the framing and the

adoption of the Judiciary Act of 1789, the law that created the federal court system.

Unlike today's Congress, the First Congress did not rely on committees of its members to do most of its work. Most legislative business was carried out on the floor of each house. Every now and then, the House or Senate would appoint a *select* committee. Its members would go off, discuss the question "committed" to them, and report back to the full house. The select committee would then dissolve. Only gradually did the House and Senate come to appoint *standing* (permanent) committees of members to carry out certain regular functions. Standing committees did not become a central feature of the Congressional process until the early nineteenth century.

In the House, Representative Madison won general recognition as the leading member. The House had a presiding officer, the Speaker, but all the first Speaker, Frederick Augustus Muhlenberg of Pennsylvania, had to do was to preside over the meetings of the House. Under Madison's guidance, the House proposed bills setting up taxes and customs regulations, creating the executive departments of government, and, most far-reaching of all, proposing constitutional amendments.

In the ratification fight of 1787–1788, many Americans had demanded that the Constitution be amended to include a list of individual rights that the federal government could not violate. Under pressure from Jefferson, and his own growing belief that amendments were necessary, Madison took the lead in proposing such amendments and ramming them through Congress. Representative Fisher Ames of Massachusetts thought that Madison was just making a bid for popularity, but Madison was unshakable in his determination to win the day for his amendments. In September 1789, at the end of its first session, the First Congress finally agreed on twelve proposed amendments and sent them to the states for ratification. After slightly more than two years, ten of the twelve, which we call the Bill of Rights, became part of the Constitution. (The other two, concerning House membership and compensation to members of Congress, have never been adopted.)

Madison also worked closely with President Washington. He helped to draft Washington's first Inaugural Address, then wrote the House's reply to the President, and finally wrote Washington's answer to the House's reply to the President's speech. The President respected Madison and valued his friendship and advice. Madison returned this respect. In those early days, the President and Congress worked in careful partnership.

In its second and third sessions, the First Congress turned its attention to the most pressing problem affecting the new government—debt. The United States and the states had run up staggering debts throughout the Revolution by borrowing money to pay for weapons, powder, uniforms, bandages, and other supplies for the Continental Army and to keep the Confederation going. How were these debts to be handled? Should the new nation try to pay them off? What could be done?

Congress had created the Treasury Department, and President Washington had appointed Alexander Hamilton as the first Secretary of the Treasury. Hamilton looked upon the debt crisis as a great opportunity to put into practice economic theories he had been working on for months. His economic policies, set forth in eloquent and closely reasoned reports, hit the First Congress like a bomb. The Senators and Representatives were astonished at his boldness.

Hamilton proposed that the United States assume the states' debts and consolidate them with the federal debt. He also proposed that Congress create a national bank to regulate the value of federal money and to stimulate investments. In a complex system of transactions, the debt would be turned into an engine to stimulate the economy, to strengthen the government of the United States, and to ensure that the commercial interests and the wealthy would become firm friends of the new government.

Hamilton's policies outraged many members of the House and Senate, who argued that he was "selling the government out" to the rich and powerful. Even James Madison, who had been Hamilton's friend and ally in the struggle to win adoption of the Constitution in 1787–1788, disapproved. Madison tried to lead the House in opposition to Hamilton's proposals but was defeated. A complicated series of deals between the Administration and Representatives and Senators from Pennsylvania and Virginia resulted in the adoption of Hamilton's programs in exchange for moving the capital to Philadelphia for ten years and then to a permanent site on the banks of the Potomac River between Virginia and Maryland. These clashes were important, for they marked the beginning of a development that no one had foreseen: the rise of political parties.

Washington, Madison, Hamilton, and their contemporaries feared and distrusted parties. They believed that parties were combinations of persons who did not have the general interest of society at heart and that these groups' pursuit of their own selfish interests could damage or even destroy a free, republican government. But these political leaders turned out to be wrong. Parties have become loose, broad-based coalitions of various sorts of people who have special interests to pursue but who also agree on general principles that the government should embody and goals that it should carry out. And parties soon became central to the way that Congress does its job.

CHAPTER THREE

DEBATE AND DISCORD

The great achievement of the First Congress (1789–1791) was to channel American politics within the matrix set up by the Constitution. For the next two decades, the new national political system also adapted itself to the growing system of political parties, and Congress had a major role in this process. Even so, the people and the politicians of the time only gradually accepted the idea that political parties were becoming necessary to the smooth working of government under the Constitution.

Two political parties emerged during the 1790s, the Federalists and the Republicans.

The *Federalists*—who were different from the supporters of the Constitution in the ratification contests of 1787–1788—supported a broad reading of the Constitution that would confer generous grants of power on the federal government. They enthusiastically argued that the "elastic clause" granted the federal government all powers and responsibilities not strictly forbidden to it by the Constitution. They also feared too much democracy, worrying that the horrors of the French Revolution might be unleashed in the United States. Because they were opposed to the excesses of the French Revolution, the Federalists favored either keeping the United States neutral in the rivalry and wars between France and England then taking place or actively allying with England. Washington, Adams, Hamilton, and John Jay were leading Federalists.

The *Republicans* believed that the Constitution should be read narrowly, to give the United States only those powers specifically mentioned in the Constitution. They disliked the Federalist reliance on the "elastic clause." The Republicans claimed that the Federalists favored some form of kingship, or monarchy, for America. The Republicans also applauded the French Revolution's overthrow of monarchy and made excuses for the excesses of the Revolution. They wanted the United States to honor its 1778 treaty with France, even though the French had executed Louis XVI, the king who had agreed to that treaty. Jefferson, Madison, Monroe, and George Clinton of New York were leading Republicans.

Party politics flared repeatedly in the halls of Congress. One controversy set major precedents for relations between Congress and the President in the matter of Congressional investigations. Federal land policy encouraged speculators to buy land in the Northwest Territories (present-day Ohio), where they had no business interfering with peaceful Indians. In late 1791 and early 1792, two detachments of federal soldiers sent to protect these speculators and settlers were cut to pieces by enraged Indians. Congress immediately called for an investigation, and the first House investigating committee was appointed. It asked President Washington to turn over papers and other records pertaining to the military missions that had ended so disastrously. The President and his advisers agreed to turn over some documents to the House committee but claimed the right to decide what documents should not be turned over, "the disclosure of which would endanger the public." Based on the documents the Administration did provide, Congress charged that corruption among the officials assigned to buy military supplies for federal troops was a major cause of the military disasters in Ohio. This accusation, aimed at the Treasury Department led by Secretary Hamilton, infuriated Hamilton and his supporters, and the first Congressional investigation helped to feed the split between the parties.

A second issue resulted in the first Presidential veto of a bill passed by Congress. President Washington received a highly technical compromise bill on reapportioning the House of Representatives (allotting seats in the House to states based on changing population) that seemed to be unconstitutional. He instructed Secretary of State Jefferson and Attorney General Edmund Randolph to work with Madison to prepare a veto message. Although some members of Congress were furious, there was no challenge to the veto. Washington's veto is notable also because it set a precedent for future Presidents to veto bills only on constitutional grounds—a precedent that lasted for nearly half a century.

A dispute about the Senate's way of conducting its business set another precedent. In 1793, when the Swiss-born Albert Gallatin of Pennsylvania was elected to the Senate, Federalist Senators began a campaign to oust him. They claimed that he had not been a citizen of the United States long enough to be a Senator. The Senate realized that if the proceedings on Gallatin took place behind closed doors, Gallatin's supporters could charge that a conspiracy had stolen his election. So the Senate opened its proceedings to the view of the press and the public for the first time. After the Senators voted to deny Gallatin his seat, they decided to continue meeting in public, as the House had been doing since 1789.

Animosity between Federalists and Republicans continued to grow through the balance of Washington's two terms as Chief Executive. Not even his unanimous re-election in 1792 could dampen party sentiment. The Whiskey Rebellion of 1794 gave Secretary Hamilton the chance to assert convincingly the authority of the federal government, but it also sowed seeds of discontent throughout the nation. In a message to Congress, President Washington denounced the activities of "democratic societies" for having helped to induce the farmers of western Pennsylvania to take arms against federal laws imposing taxes on distilling whiskey. The Federalists capitalized on Washington's outrage. The Republicans responded by reminding the Federalists that such societies had a constitutional right to organize and to publish their views.

When the treaty with Great Britain negotiated in London by Chief Justice John Jay (to normalize relations between the two countries) reached the United States in early 1795, bitterness between Federalists and Republicans reached all-time highs. Republicans charged that Chief Justice Jay had given away far too much to the British and that he was ignoring the interests of the South and the West in favor of the interests of New England and the Eastern seaports. Jay's role in this treaty made him one of the most unpopular men in the nation. It was said that he could walk at night from one end of the country to the other by the light of the fires burning him in effigy.

Even after the Senate ratified the treaty, the controversy continued. The House demanded that the President turn over papers relative to the negotiation of the treaty so it could decide whether to appropriate funds to help carry it out. Washington curtly informed the Representatives that these papers were none of their business. Ultimately, the Federalists won the day, thanks to the impassioned eloquence of Federalist Representative Fisher Ames. The former Speaker of the House, Frederick Muhlenberg, voted for the treaty even though he was a Republican. As a result, his angered brother-in-law stabbed him, and Muhlenberg lost his bid for re-election to the House.

Washington retired from the Presidency, sick at heart and exhausted by the violence of party politics. His Farewell

Address, published in newspapers in September 1796, voiced his disgust at partisanship, which did nothing to endear him to the Republicans. The 1796 Presidential election did little to calm things down, either. The next four years, President John Adams's lone term in office, were the roughest yet for the new government.

Adams tried to walk a narrow line between the warring powers of Europe. But when French naval vessels carried out assaults on American ships, Adams sent a three-man delegation to Paris to try to stop the attacks. As Congress waited for news from France, tempers worsened. In fact, on January 1, 1798, Representative Matthew Lyon of Vermont, a frontier Republican, spit a stream of tobacco juice into the face of Federalist Representative Roger Griswold of Connecticut. After weeks of watching the House wrangle over its rules of discipline, Griswold literally took measures into his own hands and attacked Lyon with a hickory cane. Lyon picked up the House's fire tongs, and the two men whacked and swore at each other as other Representatives whooped and applauded. A motion to expel both men was defeated. But the Griswold-Lyon fight in the House suggested to worried Americans that partisan politics was getting so hot it might never cool down.

When news from Adams's representatives in France arrived in Philadelphia, the nation became furious. Corrupt French diplomats had declined to listen to the Americans' suggestions unless they first received bribes. The three Americans indignantly refused. Adams called for Congress to adopt defense measures and to back an undeclared naval war with France. Congress also passed—and the President signed—the Alien and Sedition Acts, harsh laws punishing criticism of the government. Federalists were delighted. Republicans, who expected to be the targets of these new laws, were cast into gloom. But the expected call for a congressional declaration of war never came.

Adams then realized that the French were willing to work matters out. And he discovered that his advisers were serving their idol and chief Hamilton rather than the President of the United States. In 1799, the President surprised the nation by opening new talks with the French; the next year, he cleaned out the "vipers" in his Cabinet. He saved the nation from a disastrous war but in doing so cost himself the election of 1800.

By this time, informal gatherings of party members in Congress—*caucuses*—selected the parties' Presidential and Vice Presidential candidates. The Federalists renominated Adams, but the split in the party was so serious that Hamilton and his colleagues schemed to bury the President in the electoral votes and elect Vice Presidential candidate Charles C. Pinckney of South Carolina the new President. Hamilton's strategy backfired, however, and the Republicans triumphed.

The victorious Republicans had made a major mistake, however: They had not made sure that Thomas Jefferson, their Presidential candidate (and Adams's Vice President), would get more electoral votes than their Vice Presidential candidate, Aaron Burr of New York. The two men ended up tied with seventy-three votes each. Under the Constitution, the House of Representatives, voting by states, had the job of sorting out a tie vote in the Electoral College. It took the Representatives several weeks and thirty-six ballots to decide on Jefferson. Hamilton privately urged Federalist Representatives to vote for the Republican Jefferson, and Burr's continued silence persuaded the House that he was too ambitious to be trusted.

Jefferson's election, in February 1801, only a few days before Inauguration Day (then in March), persuaded Congress to overhaul the Electoral College. Congress wrote the Twelfth Amendment, which requires the Electoral College to cast separate votes for Presidential and Vice Presidential candidates. This Amendment was ratified in time for the Presiden-

tial election of 1804. It was the first constitutional amendment proposed in the nation's permanent capital.

The new federal capital city, Washington, D.C., was
"ready" in 1800, and the government moved glumly to the
swampy, mosquito-infested, humid place. It was there that
the Jefferson-Burr deadlock of 1800 was settled and that the
nation and the world witnessed the first peaceful transition
from one party to another under the Constitution. The
Republicans had swept both the Presidency and Congress.
They controlled both the Senate and the House, leaving the
disgruntled Federalists ensconced in the judiciary.

President Jefferson worked closely at first with the new
Speaker of the House, Nathaniel Macon of North Carolina,
and with Macon's choice to head the important House Ways
and Means Committee (the committee in charge of taxation
bills), Virginian Representative John Randolph of Roanoke.
Randolph was a distant cousin of the President, but the two
men loathed each other. Randolph was eccentric to the point
of mental imbalance, and other Representatives soon learned
to fear the lash of his tongue.

Jefferson soon mastered a major change in the way that
Congress did its business. As the ranks of the House and
Senate swelled with Representatives and Senators from new
states, Congress created standing committees. These committees acted almost as miniature legislatures, discussing and
proposing bills, which were then debated and voted on by the
full House and Senate. The creation of committees made the
work of Congress somewhat more efficient. It also gave power
to the Speaker of the House, who would pick the chairmen
of the committees based on party loyalty. (The Senate elected
its committees and chairmen by secret ballot, preserving the
independence of its members.) Jefferson worked with committee chairmen, but he also chose informal "agents" from the
ranks of the House and Senate to watch over Administration
interests.

In the winter of 1801, the outgoing Federalist Congress had created dozens of new federal judgeships, and President Adams had appointed Federalists to these posts. A wrangle over one of these appointments led to the first decision by the Supreme Court striking down an act of Congress as unconstitutional—an exercise of *judicial review*. The 1803 case of *Marbury v. Madison* focused on a technical point of the jurisdiction of the Supreme Court in a section of the Judiciary Act of 1789, but President Jefferson and his Republican colleagues in Congress realized that the decision had far-reaching significance. They were outraged by Chief Justice John Marshall's claim that the Court had the power to strike down a statute as unconstitutional. They also resented that the Federalists had planted themselves in the federal courts. They determined to wage war on the Federalist judiciary. Their chosen weapon was impeachment.

Congress targeted a senile, drunken New Hampshire federal district judge, John Pickering. He never knew what hit him. The House impeached him, and the Senate removed him from office. Nobody could explain what his impeachable offense was. One Republican in the House declared that impeachment was simply an inquiry by Congress whether a federal office might better be filled by someone other than the current official.

The House then went after old, fat Samuel Chase, a Justice of the Supreme Court. He had enraged Republicans by his gleeful conduct of trials for violations of the hated Sedition Act. Chase was impeached by the House, but the Senate trial in 1805 was another matter. For one thing, Representative John Randolph of Roanoke, the "manager" (that is, prosecutor) of the Chase impeachment, was erratic and undependable. For another, Vice President Aaron Burr presided over the trial. Burr had never overcome Jefferson's distrust of him following the election of 1800. He also had disgraced himself and destroyed his career by killing Alexander Hamilton in a duel. But Burr was determined to conduct the trial of Justice Chase honorably and fairly. He managed the Senate trial so well, in fact, that he won approval of all but his bitterest foes. The impeachment process was stopped dead when the Senate acquitted Justice Chase on March 1, 1805. Three days later, Vice President Burr made a farewell speech to the Senate: "This House, is a sanctuary; a citadel of law, of order, and of liberty; and it is here, in this exalted refuge, here, if any-where, will resistance be made to the storms of political phrensy and the silent arts of corruption; and, if the Consti-tution be destined ever to perish by the sacrilegious hands of the demagogue or the usurper, which God avert, its expiring agonies will be witnessed on this floor."

In President Jefferson's second term, Representative John Randolph of Roanoke was toppled from power as the chair-man of the House Ways and Means Committee. His long-suffering colleagues had grown impatient with Randolph's sloppy methods of running the committee and his increasingly strange behavior. Speaker Macon bowed to pressure from the rank-and-file members and appointed another House member to the chairmanship. The enraged Randolph drew around himself a group of like-minded Representatives and bedeviled Jefferson and his successor, James Madison.

Randolph's faction contributed to the difficulty that Con-gress and Madison had with each other in Madison's first term. Neither house had strong leadership, and the President was not providing guidance, either. As the government floun-dered, the United States drifted toward war with Great Britain over British attacks on American shipping during its wars with Napoleonic France.

The leadership question in the House was settled as if by a stroke of lightning at the end of 1811. Henry Clay of Ken-tucky, who had served briefly in the Senate (though he was several months too young) and had made a prodigious repu-tation for himself as an orator and political wheeler-dealer, entered the House as a freshman member and on the first day captured the Speakership. Clay became one of the most vigorous, able, and dynamic Speakers in the history of the House. He once explained his methods: "Decide, decide promptly, and never give your reasons for your decision. The House will sustain your decisions, but there will always be men to cavil and quarrel about your reasons."

The free-living, hard-drinking Speaker and a group of other young Representatives from the South and West agitated fiercely for war against Great Britain. They wanted to punish slurs on national honor and to acquire Canada for the United States. One of these "war hawks" was John C. Calhoun, a brilliant, humorless Representative from South Carolina. Because of the war hawks' pressure and because he believed that war with England was necessary to defend the Constitution, President Madison asked Congress for a declaration of war in 1812. Congress swiftly gave him what he—and they— wanted.

The War of 1812 was a mixed bag for the United States. After a series of early naval victories, the U.S. Navy found itself bottled up in American harbors by an unbreakable British blockade. On land, advantages seesawed back and forth. The most humiliating moment came in 1814, when the British landed a force that burned Washington, D.C. Legend has it that their commanding officer stood on the Speaker's chair in the Capitol and asked his men, "Shall this citadel of Yankee democracy be burned?" Congress returned to find that the Capitol was a smoke-blackened ruin. The British had stolen or destroyed the mace of the House, the symbol of its official dignity. The Senate wing was nothing but piles of timber and ash. Rebuilding began at once, but the damage to the pride of Congress and the nation took longer to heal.

Congress was in a state of shock. Its members could not agree on even the most necessary measures. The government was all but paralyzed. New England legislators such as Representative Daniel Webster of New Hampshire talked angrily of the possibility that their states might leave the Union to end their role in the useless war.

With the end of the war in early 1815, however, the nation and Congress recovered some measure of spirit and enterprise. A new generation of leaders was emerging. Its chief members were Clay, Calhoun, and Webster.

CHAPTER FOUR

THE AGE OF GIANTS

For three decades, from the 1820s to the 1850s, Henry Clay, John C. Calhoun, and Daniel Webster dominated American politics. They had begun their careers at the same time in the House of Representatives in the Twelfth Congress, in 1811. But it was not until all three men entered the Senate that the "golden age" of American legislative politics began.

This new age also witnessed major changes in political parties and the political process. The end of the War of 1812 brought with it the disintegration of the Federalist Party. But the Republican Party did not long survive its old adversary. It split into several factions during the 1824 election. John Quincy Adams of Massachusetts, President Monroe's Secretary of State and the son of former President John Adams, was the standard-bearer of the National Republicans. General Andrew Jackson, a military hero of the War of 1812 and of many skirmishes with Indians, was the candidate of a group that began to call itself Democrats. The Congressional Republican caucus named Senator William Crawford its candidate, but Crawford suffered a series of strokes, which left him crippled and nearly blind. (Crawford was the last Presidential candidate named by a Congressional caucus.) And Senator Henry Clay was a candidate as well.

The four candidates so divided the electoral votes that no one man received a majority, and the election landed in the House. Clay threw his support to John Quincy Adams, who thus was able to edge out the front-runner, General Jackson. When President Adams chose Clay to be his Secretary of State, Jacksonians charged that a "corrupt" bargain had taken place. Four years later, they triumphantly swept Adams out of the White House and Jackson in. The opposition to Jackson reorganized as a new political party to counter Jackson's Democrats. They called themselves the Whigs, taking the name from the old English political party associated with the defense of political liberty.

Congress adjusted itself to this new party system. The House of Representatives and the Senate had begun to work out a rough division of roles. The House tended to direct the grinding business of legislation, and the Senate emerged as the forum of debate. Meeting in a chamber with superb acoustics, Senators could hold their colleagues and packed galleries of visitors spellbound for hours or even days. Oratory in the first half of the nineteenth century was as entertaining as a hard-fought World Series or popular television program can be today. And the "great triumvirate," as historian Merrill Peterson has dubbed Clay, Calhoun, and Webster, were the greatest of the Senate's orators.

Clay, Webster, and Calhoun had weighty subjects to hold forth on. President Andrew Jackson's fiery temper and rough-edged brand of politics were lightning rods for Senatorial criticism. He was not willing to defer to Congress, as his predecessors had been. He was his own man and ruthlessly used the powers of the Presidency to advance his own agenda and to hammer at Congress when it stood in his way. "Old Hickory" discarded the precedent, established by George Washington, of limiting the use of the Presidential veto to constitutional grounds. Jackson vetoed bills merely because he disagreed with them, and he made his vetoes stick. He resisted Congressional attempts to censure him, and he took delight in skewering his enemies in the House and the Senate.

Another issue worthy of these great debates was slavery. The delegates to the Federal Convention had sidestepped the problem, hoping it would fade away on its own. But slavery persisted—a smoldering bomb waiting for the moment to explode. Henry Clay helped to defuse the first such potential explosion by hammering together the Missouri Compromise in 1820. Under the Missouri Compromise, Missouri was allowed to enter the Union as a slave state, and Maine, once part of Massachusetts, came in as a free state. These two new states preserved the balance of power in the Senate between free states and slave states. A line drawn across the rest of the Union at latitude 36° 30' North marked off the regions where new states would be free (north of the line) or slave (south of the line), again to preserve the balance of power.

A third great issue was the character of the Union. Was the Constitution the creation of the states? Did a state have authority to decide which federal laws would be valid within its borders and which would not? Did a state have the right to choose to leave the Union? Southern Senators such as Robert Y. Hayne of South Carolina answered these questions "Yes." In a major speech on the floor of the Senate in 1830, Hayne voiced the "state sovereignty" theory of the Constitution shared by Calhoun and other Southerners. By this time, Calhoun had become Vice President under Jackson. (He had also been John Quincy Adams's Vice President.) He could take no part in the debate, but he nodded approvingly as Hayne addressed the Senate. In response to Hayne, Daniel Webster, now a Senator from Massachusetts, made a powerful and eloquent plea in favor of "the people's Constitution." The Constitution, Webster declared, was created by the People of the United States; by adopting it, the People created both a national government superior to the states and a permanent Union.

Senators Hayne and Webster revived a dispute, going back to the framing of the Constitution in 1787, that would persist for decades. Soon, however, Hayne stepped aside as the spokesman for state power in favor of his hero, John C. Calhoun. Calhoun resigned from the Vice Presidency in early 1832 to protest President Jackson's unflinching support for federal power against the "rights" of South Carolina. He was sent to the Senate by the South Carolina legislature to speak for its interests and to argue for the "state compact" theory of the Constitution.

The House, too, had its say about such issues as slavery and the Union. Former President John Quincy Adams had broken precedent by returning to public life in 1830 as a Whig Representative from Massachusetts. He soon emerged as a vigorous defender of the *right of petition.*

Americans of all points of views had long sent petitions to Congress setting forth their hopes for legislation, their goals for national development, or their attacks on national policy. Fearing the divisive effect of the slavery issue, the House leadership proposed a rule barring any member from presenting a petition having to do with slavery. Adams fought a lonely and energetic eight-year campaign in the House against this "gag rule," claiming that it violated the First Amendment. He finally triumphed, despite at least one attempt by the House to censure him.

But it was the Senate that tended to attract popular attention, and it was the three great men of their time who were most interesting to the nation. Each man represented one of the three great sections of the nation: Clay, the West; Webster, the North; and Calhoun, the South. Clay was known as the "Great Compromiser," for his role in pulling together the Missouri Compromise that saved the Union in 1820. He also became known for his dream of the *American system*—a vast network of roads, bridges, and other internal improvements paid for by the federal government and intended to help knit the Union together and to foster the growth of American industries to compete with Europe. Webster, allied with Clay in his campaigns for internal improvements, was also known as the defender of the Union. Calhoun, the voice of the South and its greatest intellectual strategist, hammered home his theory that the Constitution was—and had to be—a compact among the states, not a charter of government adopted by the people of the United States.

The Union in this period was like a fragile piece of china balanced on a knife's edge. Men of all political stripes watched it cautiously, shuddering at each tremor of the ground. It was in the halls of Congress that each new tremor was most carefully monitored, and where each new crisis was faced.

Even issues that did not on the surface have a clear connection to slavery and the Union could ignite the powder keg. Most disturbing was the matter of acquiring new territory. Each such acquisition raised the question of how the territories would be organized: Would they become free states or slave states? Northerners asked whether a push to acquire territory, by purchase or the threat of force or even war, was simply a bid to get more territory in which slavery could be expanded. Southerners retorted that Northern opposition to the acquisition of more territory clearly showed Northern hostility to slavery by choking off needed room for growth.

The Mexican War of 1846–1848 became the most sensitive territorial issue by far. The Whigs opposed the war with great bitterness, denouncing it as robbery. A young first-term Representative from Illinois named Abraham Lincoln implied that President James K. Polk (the only Speaker of the House ever to be a successful candidate for President) had deliberately provoked war with Mexico. Other Whigs joined in. (John Quincy Adams suffered a fatal stroke on the floor of the

House in early 1848 as he waited impatiently to speak against the war.) The Whigs also raised the antislavery issue. Representative David Wilmot of Pennsylvania attached to a necessary appropriations bill a provision barring the spread of slavery into any territories acquired as a result of the war. The Wilmot Proviso, as it was called, resurfaced again and again but always met defeat. Still, each reappearance raised the dread issue of slavery.

One consequence of the growing importance of the slavery issue was a change in the method of organization of the Senate. Senators had elected their committees and their committee chairmen by secret ballot. In December 1846, it was agreed that party caucuses would choose the members of the committees and that the Senate would accept these arrangements. This was the seed of the *seniority system*: Senators who had served longest would get first choices of committee assignments. It was also a way for the leadership of both parties to control the assignment of Senators to committees that might have explosive consequences for the slavery issue.

At the end of the Mexican War, the United States acquired for $15 million—by the Treaty of Guadalupe Hidalgo—more than half of Mexico's territory: a vast area of the present Southwest from Texas to California, which included most of what is now Colorado, Utah, Nevada, New Mexico, and Arizona. This new territory, and the recurrent threat of the Wilmot Proviso, led to one of the greatest periods in the history of the Senate. On February 5 and 6, 1850, Henry Clay, now seventy-three years old, began the debate with a set of compromise proposals designed to save the Union. He suggested that the Republic of California join the Union as a free state. (Its constitution already prohibited slavery.) He also proposed a series of concessions demanded by Southern Senators as the price for California's admission to the Union.

On March 4, John C. Calhoun, speaking for the die-hard

Southern Senators, replied to Clay. The "Iron Man" was emaciated, racked with tuberculosis, and too frail to give his own speech. His eyes burned somberly as he listened to Senator James M. Mason of Virginia read his address. Calhoun offered no quarter to Clay or to anyone else from the North or West. His last speech was an unbending call for Southern unity. Every last Southern condition for compromise must be met. Calhoun rejected Clay's compromise proposal and threatened that the Southern states would leave the Union, or *secede*, if his terms were not met.

Three days later, Daniel Webster arose to reply to Calhoun and to endorse Clay's compromise plan. The "Seventh of March" speech is now regarded as Webster's greatest, but at the time he gravely injured his standing in the eyes of Northern abolitionists (who wanted to end slavery). Point by point, Webster explained and endorsed Clay's compromise proposal and sadly rejected Calhoun's threats of disunion. He set the tone of his speech with his opening lines: "I wish to speak today not as a Massachusetts man, nor as a Northern man, but as an American. . . . I speak today for the preservation of the Union. 'Hear me for my cause.' "

Within four weeks, Calhoun was dead, the first of the Great Triumvirate to pass from the scene. He was spared one of the ugliest and silliest scenes in the history of the Senate. Senators' tempers had become so frayed that many carried knives, small pistols, and other weapons for self-defense. Senator Henry S. Foote of Mississippi, a short, violent-tempered man, had gotten into a wrestling match with one Northern Senator and had threatened to hang another. Tall, bluff Senator Thomas Hart Benton of Missouri, who was a much greater man and Senator than he appears to be in this incident, had frequently mocked Foote's readiness to fight duels. In an angry exchange of words, Benton kept advancing on Foote. Foote suddenly drew a pistol. Benton bellowed, "Let him fire! Stand out of the way! Let the assassin fire!"

Senator Henry Clay (Whig–Kentucky) holds his colleagues spellbound during his memorable appeal for a compromise on slavery. Senator Daniel Webster (Whig–Massachusetts) sits at the left, holding his head. Senator John C. Calhoun (Democrat– South Carolina) stands third from the right. Clay, Webster, and Calhoun were known as the Great Triumvirate.

Other Senators separated Benton and Foote, and the Mississippian explained that he had assumed that the Missourian was armed.

By the end of September, the several bills making up Clay's Compromise of 1850 were finally voted into law and signed by President Millard Fillmore. Within two years, both Clay and Webster were also dead. An age of giants had come to an end. It seemed at first that the giants had taken the spectre of disunion over slavery to the grave with them, but such was not to be the case.

CHAPTER FIVE

THE HOUSE—AND SENATE—DIVIDED

In the 1850s, the Whig Party faded away, disintegrating as completely as had the Federalists in the late 1810s. A short-lived Free Soil Party, whose platform opposed slavery, gave way to an organization that brought together Free-Soilers, abandoned Whigs, and other politicians bent on preserving the Union and opposing the "slavocracy." They called themselves the Republicans, after the old party founded by Jefferson and Madison in the 1790s. They claimed to be the true heirs of the Jeffersonian commitment to the rights of human beings (although Jefferson and Madison had owned slaves). By 1856, the Republicans had become a permanent political force.

The issue of slavery became ever more divisive in the 1850s. Many political observers feared that the successors of Clay, Calhoun, and Webster lacked the will or the ingenuity to carry on the process of compromise.

In 1854, the territories of Kansas and Nebraska hovered on the brink of statehood. Would they enter the Union as free states or slave states? The controversy focused on Kansas because it was below the old line drawn by the Missouri Compromise and thus ordinarily would be classified as a slave state. But nobody believed that this mechanical solution would work. Abolitionists in the North and West squared off against proslavery agitators in the South and pro-Southern "doughface" Democrats in the other sections.

Senator Stephen A. Douglas (Democrat–Illinois) was at the storm center of the Kansas crisis. The tiny, pugnacious man had been nicknamed "the Little Giant" because of his ferocious speaking style. He thought he had the answer, and he was ambitious enough to hope that it would propel him into the Presidency.

Douglas argued that Congress could not—and should not—impose a solution to the Kansas crisis. Why not let the people of the territory decide the issue for themselves by majority vote? Douglas called this solution *popular sovereignty*. It sounded simple, and it sounded as if it were a principled solution. But there was a problem. Both proslavery and antislavery organizations mustered hundreds of like-minded settlers to the Kansas territory to stack the outcome of the election. Outbreaks of violence, including bloody massacres of unarmed settlers, made all previous disputes over slavery look like tea parties.

The halls of Congress once again saw real and threatened bloodshed. Members of the House and Senate who knew their Shakespeare even feared that one of their number might be murdered in the Capitol, just as Julius Caesar had been murdered by Senators in Rome nearly two thousand years before. The fate of Senator Charles Sumner seemed to bear out these concerns.

Sumner, a Massachusetts Republican, was a great orator who fiercely opposed slavery. In a speech to the Senate on the subject of "Bleeding Kansas," he went out of his way to attack Southern Senators who were members of the "slave oligarchy." Among Sumner's targets was the absent Andrew P. Butler of South Carolina. Butler's nephew, Representative Preston Brooks, swore vengeance on Sumner.

On May 22, 1856, Brooks and a South Carolina colleague, Representative Laurence M. Keitt, entered the Senate Chamber. Members of each house regularly visited each other's chambers, so no one took much notice. Both Brooks and Keitt had wooden canes in hand. The Senate had adjourned for the day, and Sumner was writing at his desk. He did not notice the two Representatives approaching him from behind. Brooks raised his cane and slammed it down again and again across the Senator's head and shoulders. Keitt stood guard, brandishing his cane to prevent any other Senator from coming to Sumner's aid. Sumner struggled helplessly, but his long legs were held in place by his desk, and he could not get out of the range of Brooks's murderous assault. Finally, with a convulsive effort, Sumner ripped his desk from where it was bolted to the floor and collapsed across its top. Brooks and Keitt walked from the Senate Chamber, shaking hands with several Southern Senators on the way out. Other Senators carried Sumner's senseless body from the chamber.

Sumner was so badly injured by the attack that he could not return to the Senate for two years. The Massachusetts legislature refused to select a replacement; Sumner's seat would be waiting for him whenever he was strong enough to return. Brooks received congratulations from all over the South and several canes to replace the one he had broken over Sumner's back. The Democratic leadership in the Senate blocked any investigation of the incident. In the House, Republicans moved to expel Brooks and Keitt, but the motion did not get the two-thirds vote needed for adoption. Brooks and Keitt nonetheless resigned, only to be re-elected in triumph.

"Bleeding Kansas" dominated American politics. Even the Supreme Court tried to solve the slavery issue. But the attempt to transform the issue into a constitutional question (and settle it by a final decision of the Justices) backfired. The *Dred Scott* decision held that slavery was protected by the

Constitution and that Congress could not interfere with it anywhere in the United States. Southerners were delighted, but Northerners were outraged. Moderates on the issue piously begged the nation to uphold the Court's decision but refused to comment on the merits of the decision.

The outcome of Senator Douglas's "popular sovereignty" proposal was predictable: two governments in Kansas—one favoring slavery, the other opposing it. Each claimed to be the legitimate state government. Each government had its supporters in Congress. By now, Douglas realized that his bid to solve the slavery question had failed completely. He denounced the proslavery government and its "constitution" as "a trick, a fraud upon the rights of the people." But he failed to defeat the proslavery forces led by the unbending Senator Jefferson Davis (Democrat–Mississippi). Davis rammed through the Senate a bill admitting Kansas to the Union as a slave state.

When the House got the Senate bill, the Representatives got into shouting matches, fist fights, and even a full-fledged brawl. The members rejected the Senate bill, and leaders of the House and Senate began a long but fruitless quest for a compromise. The Kansas matter simmered without a solution until after the Civil War broke out, in 1861.

In 1858, Senator Douglas found himself in the political fight of his life. He was running for another term in the Senate against Republican challenger Abraham Lincoln, a Springfield lawyer and former Representative. The state legislature elected Senators, but the outcome of its vote was a strict party matter. Lincoln and Douglas agreed to debate each other several times throughout Illinois. The debates were dominated by slavery, Kansas, and *Dred Scott*. They became hugely popular events, attracting hundreds of spectators and coverage by the newspapers. The Democrats carried the state legislature, and Douglas was re-elected. But the debates made Lincoln a national figure and a major contender for the Republican Presidential nomination in 1860. They also had injured Douglas's hopes for the Presidency. The Little Giant was hard-pressed to explain how he could support popular sovereignty and yet endorse the Supreme Court's *Dred Scott* decision. Southern Democrats were furious with him, and Northerners grew to distrust him.

By 1860, Congress was stalemated between North and South. National attention focused on the Presidential election. The Democrats split into three factions. Proslavery Democrats settled on Senator John C. Breckinridge of Kentucky. Northern antislavery and moderate Democrats rallied behind Stephen Douglas. And old-line politicians who still wanted to compromise the slavery issue endorsed former Senator John Bell of Tennessee, who ran on the Constitutional Union ticket. Abraham Lincoln became the Republican Presidential candidate as his managers outmaneuvered the abolitionist front-runner, Governor William Seward of New York, in the nominating convention in Chicago, Illinois.

The three-way Democratic split handed the election to the Republicans. Lincoln swept the electoral votes but got only a plurality of the popular vote (that is, he got more votes—40 percent—than any other candidate but fewer than half of the total). Southern politicians feared what would happen once Lincoln became President. Southern states talked about seceding from the Union. President James Buchanan timidly declared that no state had the right to secede but that the federal government could not prevent a state from seceding if it chose to do so. (He was like the driver of an automobile who, seeing that an accident is about to happen, takes his hands off the steering wheel and closes his eyes.)

Congress tried desperately to prevent the developing crisis, but all efforts at compromise conventions failed. In January 1861, five Southern states voted to leave the Union. On January 21, five Southern Senators dramatically filed out of the Senate Chamber. The last to leave was Mississippi's

Jefferson Davis, who addressed his colleagues: "I am sure I feel no hostility toward you, Senators from the North. I am sure there is not one of you, whatever sharp discussion there may have been between us, to whom I cannot now say, in the presence of my God, I wish you well." As Davis walked from the chamber, Senators and onlookers wept quietly.

What did secession mean? other Senators and Representatives wondered, as one by one their Southern colleagues left for home. Was this just another Southern power play? Most

Collection of L. Allen MacLean

Jefferson Davis (Democrat–Mississippi), a former Secretary of War, took part in the first parade of Senators from the eleven seceding Southern states out of the upper house in early 1861. He helped to set up the "Confederate States of America" and served as the Confederacy's only president. After the Civil War, Davis was held in chains in a federal military prison (1865–1867). He was given a hero's funeral in New Orleans in 1889.

politicians, including President-elect Lincoln, were not sure whether to take seriously the newly organized "Confederate States of America," whose president was Jefferson Davis. In fact, the depleted Congress carried on business as usual for three months, relying on the absence of the Southern members to push through tariff bills and the bills admitting Kansas as a free state.

President Lincoln warned the South in his First Inaugural Address, on March 4, that he would be true to his constitutional duty to preserve the Union. Confederate forces demanded that the federal government abandon all its military posts in the seceded states. Lincoln refused.

The symbol of the confrontation was Fort Sumter, in the harbor of Charleston, South Carolina. On April 12, 1861, Confederate units fired on Fort Sumter. These were the opening shots of the Civil War. Because the old Congress had adjourned on March 4 and the new Congress was not scheduled to convene until fall, Lincoln considered himself free to make federal policy on the secession crisis. He issued a call for 10,000 volunteer soldiers and summoned federal soldiers to defend the capital. The first units to arrive were housed in the Capitol's basement. The building soon filled with the smell of bread baking to feed the troops.

Lincoln then called Congress to a special session to begin on July 4. On that date, he reported on the measures he had taken against the South, and Congress endorsed his policies. At first, the two branches worked in harmony, but signs of trouble were on the horizon.

Many Senators and Representatives denounced the Administration for being slow, hesitant, and lackadaisical. They had gone off to watch the first major battle of the war, at Bull Run, Virginia, as if they were going to a picnic. But the Confederate soldiers routed the Union forces, and the Congressional onlookers had to flee for their lives. A later battle claimed the life of the popular Oregon Senator Edward Baker, who had enlisted as a Major in the Union Army. Baker, a Republican and a close friend of the President, was shot dead on the field as horrified friends and colleagues looked on. Other critics in Congress were angry because Lincoln would not declare that the Union's war aims were to destroy slavery.

The President answered his critics. He pointed out that he was trying his best to force the Union commanders to fight rather than sit idly by but that it was tough and frustrating work. He also responded to abolitionist criticisms of his war aims. Lincoln's goal was to preserve the Union—whether he had to free all the slaves or none of the slaves to do it. He insisted that it was not yet time for abolition.

The recovered Senator Charles Sumner was not satisfied. Representative Thaddeus Stevens (Republican–Pennsylvania) was angered by what he saw as Lincoln's moral and military weaknesses. They spoke on behalf of a loose, quarrelsome collection of Republicans and War Democrats that some historians have lumped together as the Radicals.

The House and Senate formed the Joint Committee on the Conduct of the War, which made useful contributions to the war effort by investigating and exposing corruption in the War Department's supply operations. The President heeded the results of the Joint Committee's investigations. He replaced his Secretary of War, Simon Cameron, with War Democrat Edwin M. Stanton, a ruthless, brilliant lawyer and administrator. Stanton cleaned up the department and loyally supported the President. But the Joint Committee's other investigations, reports, demands, and suggestions soon vexed and exhausted the Administration.

As the war dragged on, Congress kept pressure on Lincoln to emancipate the slaves and abolish slavery. The House adopted a constitutional amendment to achieve these goals, but it died in the Senate. Meanwhile, the more cautious Lincoln maneuvered events so that he could act when the time was right. As the Union Army moved toward victory, another source of controversy between Congress and the President sprang up: What policy should the government adopt toward the Southern states that had tried to leave the Union? Lincoln wanted to crush the Confederacy, which he called a criminal conspiracy against the Constitution. But he disagreed with Radicals in Congress who wanted to break the South's political power and treat the region like a conquered foreign enemy. In his Second Inaugural Address, in 1865, Lincoln proposed a more lenient policy designed "to bind up the nation's wounds."

The skirmishing between Lincoln and the radical wing of his party ended abruptly less than a week after Confederate General Robert E. Lee surrendered the Army of Northern Virginia to Union General Ulysses S. Grant at Appomattox Court House in Virginia. Lincoln was murdered while attending a play at Ford's Theatre in Washington, D.C. This first Presidential assassination plunged the nation into grief. But Radical Republicans quickly saw that the assassination gave them the opportunity to impose harsh Reconstruction policies on the defeated South.

Congress got its way for the most part. It rammed through three constitutional amendments that abolished slavery (the Thirteenth Amendment, 1865), made the federal government supreme over the states in a reworking of federalism (Fourteenth Amendment, 1868), and barred discrimination against voters on the basis of race (Fifteenth, 1870). Secretary of War Edwin Stanton directed the Army's occupation of the South. The Army oversaw the defeated states' governments and established a Freedmen's Bureau to help the freed slaves.

The new President, Andrew Johnson of Tennessee, soon clashed with Congress. Johnson, the only Southern Senator who had remained loyal to the Union, was a War Democrat who nonetheless was sympathetic to the Southern whites and did not believe in racial equality. He fought the Reconstruction policy supported by Congress. He vetoed many major

Reconstruction bills, only to see them re-enacted over his veto. He then ignored or defied these laws. An outraged Thaddeus Stevens proclaimed: "Though the President is Commander-in-Chief, Congress is his commander; and, God willing, he shall obey. He and his minions shall learn that this is not a Government of kings and satraps, but a Government of the people, and that Congress is the people."

The final straw came in 1867 when Congress adopted the Tenure of Office Act. The measure required the President to get the Senate's approval before he could fire any government official whose appointment was made with the consent of the Senate. The First Congress had rejected this view in 1789, believing that the President had the right and the responsibility to fire officials on his own. Congress revived this notion to prevent President Johnson from firing Cabinet officers and other government officials who agreed with Reconstruction. Johnson defied Congress by firing Secretary of War Stanton even after the Senate had refused his request.

When Congress received word from Stanton, who had barricaded himself in his office in the War Department, the House voted to impeach the President. It appointed a seven-member special committee led by Thaddeus Stevens to draft charges, or *articles of impeachment.* Some of the charges in the eleven articles they adopted were silly, but several were well grounded in Johnson's defiance of Congress. The Tenure of Office Act crisis was the centerpiece of the impeachment effort. It did not matter that the President had only a year left in his term of office or that neither the Democrats nor the Republicans would renominate him. It was the principle that counted.

The House adopted the articles of impeachment and sent them to the Senate. The House special committee served as the managers of the impeachment before the Senate. As required by the Constitution, the Chief Justice, Salmon P. Chase, presided over the trial. Chase was a Radical Republican who nonetheless valued the rule of law. He presided over the Senate's trial with dignity and fairness, in part because he recalled the example of Vice President Aaron Burr's conduct six decades earlier during the Senate's trial of Justice Samuel Chase (no relation). The managers of the impeachment claimed that an impeachable offense was whatever the House and Senate defined it to be. President Johnson's lawyers argued that an impeachable offense had to be something serious for which you could be indicted and convicted in a court of law. Neither side prevailed clearly.

The visitors' galleries in the Senate were packed every day of the trial. Each day, two men carried the seventy-six-year-old Thaddeus Stevens into the Chamber because he was too weak to walk in with his fellow Representatives. On May 16, 1868, the Senate voted on the charges against the President. As the roll call proceeded, it became clear that twelve Democrats and six Republicans were agreed that impeachment was a legal matter, not just a political tug-of-war. They voted to acquit the President. These eighteen Senators were one-third of the Senate. The Constitution requires a two-thirds vote to convict and remove an impeached official. Thus, the pro-impeachment forces could not afford to lose a single vote. Republican Senator Edmund G. Ross of Kansas waited silently for his name to be called. As he later described it, "I looked into my open grave." When his turn came, Ross answered firmly, "Not guilty." He had saved Johnson, and he had destroyed his own political career.

If the Senate had convicted the President and removed him from office, many historians suggest that the whole balance of our constitutional system would have been altered. Ross and the six other Republican Senators believed that the Presidency itself was at risk. They voted not to save Andrew Johnson, but to save the constitutional system of separation of powers and checks and balances.

Both Congress and Andrew Johnson were relieved when he

left office in early 1869. Johnson even left town before Ulysses S. Grant's inauguration. In 1875, Johnson returned to Washington as a Senator representing his home state of Tennessee, but it had taken fifty-five ballots by the Tennessee legislature to make it happen. The only President besides John Quincy Adams to serve in Congress after his Presidency, Johnson died of a stroke less than five months after taking his seat in the upper chamber.

CHAPTER SIX

CONGRESS IN THE GILDED AGE

In 1869, Republican Ulysses S. Grant, the foremost military hero of the Civil War, took office as the eighteenth President of the United States. Nicknamed "Unconditional Surrender" Grant for his uncompromising tactics during the war, he belied his reputation for toughness within months of his inauguration. Leaders of his own party in Congress clipped his wings ruthlessly when he tried to think and act for himself in setting policy and making appointments to federal offices. Grant's surrender to Congress set the pattern for relations between the two branches for nearly a generation.

During Grant's two terms, corruption dominated American politics. Officials at all levels of government sold their influence, their judgment, and their votes. Scandals surfaced almost monthly. Congress suffered more from corruption and scandal than any other institution of government. Even the handsome, articulate Speaker of the House, James G. Blaine of Maine, was making deals with railroads and other powerful economic interests to get loans and other favors in return for his vote and support.

Even worse, the sleaziness of Congress seemed incurable.

Congressional "investigations" concealed at least as much as they were supposed to reveal. Although some notorious wrongdoers were caught and punished, others flourished.

National politics drifted. In Congress, the House took a back seat to the Senate, which quickly won the reputation of being a "millionaire's club." Wealthy men were able to bribe their way into "the nation's greatest deliberative body." It was easier to bribe a few dozen state legislators to get oneself—or a reliable stooge—into the Senate than to bribe voters to get oneself elected to the House. Public policy was made in fits and starts—if a Senator was interested enough to focus on a national problem and was able to rally enough of his colleagues to push a bill through.

During this period, agitation began, chiefly in the Midwest and West, for a constitutional amendment mandating direct election of Senators by the voters of each state rather than by the easily corruptible state legislatures. Many states already had direct-election systems, and others had enacted laws requiring their legislatures to follow the will of the people as expressed in nonbinding elections. But it would require a constitutional amendment to force *all* the states' legislatures to give up their power to choose Senators. This campaign lasted for four decades.

The fate of Republican Charles Sumner illustrates what happened to Senators who took the nation's business seriously. Still revered as the martyr of "Bleeding Kansas," Sumner was chairman of the Senate Foreign Relations Committee. He smelled corruption in a treaty that came before his committee and scuttled it—even though it was supported by President Grant. The President was relying on a trusted secretary, Orville Babcock, who had pushed the treaty in order to line his own pockets. Babcock schemed with the Republican leadership in the Senate to remove Sumner from his chairmanship. They "explained" that the committee and the Senate needed a chairman who could work closely with the Administration—that is, someone who would not make waves. The loss of his chairmanship was a terrible blow for Sumner. He died three years later, in 1874.

The nation's politics hit bottom in 1876. In the Presidential election that fall, Governor Samuel J. Tilden of New York, the Democratic Presidential nominee, faced Governor Rutherford B. Hayes of Ohio, the Republican candidate. (Hayes had been a compromise choice, selected instead of Speaker Blaine because Blaine had made powerful enemies in the party—enemies who were as corrupt as he was but who could not stomach his arrogance.) For the first time since the John Quincy Adams election over fifty years earlier, a Presidential election did not end with Election Day.

Tilden apparently had won, but Republicans challenged the results in three Southern states—Louisiana, Florida, and South Carolina—with nineteen electoral votes. With these three states up in the air, Tilden needed only one of the nineteen electoral votes to become the nineteenth President; Hayes needed them all.

Congress named a bipartisan Electoral Commission to sort the matter out. The commission included five Senators, five Representatives, and five Justices of the Supreme Court. Seven commissioners were Democrats, and seven were Republicans. Independent-minded Justice David Davis of Illinois, a longtime friend of the late President Lincoln, held the deciding vote. Illinois Republicans decided to take no chance that Davis would vote for Tilden, and they quickly elected him to the Senate. Davis felt that he had to accept the new post; thus, he had to resign from the Court and the commission. The Republican Justices then picked a loyal Republican from their ranks to replace Davis, and the commission voted, eight to seven, to give all nineteen disputed electoral votes to Hayes.

To prevent a challenge to the commission's report on the floor of Congress, Republican political leaders struck a deal with Southern Democrats. We may never know all the elements of this deal. The parties to it buried the evidence so well that even now historians cannot agree on what its terms were. We *do* know that the Southern Democrats wanted an end to the hated Reconstruction policy. They wanted to take back their state governments from the Army, Northern *carpetbaggers* (men who journeyed to the South to build new political careers for themselves based on black voters' support), and the freed slaves. The Republicans wanted Hayes in the White House. They did not care that ending Reconstruction and pulling federal soldiers out of the Southern states would leave the freed slaves without protection against their former masters. Both sides got what they wanted, and Congress voted to confirm the decision of the Electoral Commission.

The Republicans in Congress stole the Presidency from Samuel Tilden. The people had spoken, but that did not matter. Corruption had triumphed over democracy. The highest office in the land had been sold to the highest bidder.

The great American writer Mark Twain could not conceal his disgust with American politics in general, and with Congress in particular. He once described Congress as the nation's only identifiable "criminal class." He and his friend Charles Dudley Warner wrote a novel about postwar American life. Their title for the book, *The Gilded Age*, described their time as splendid in appearance but rotten under the glittering surface. Historians have adopted "the Gilded Age" as the standard nickname for this period.

But there were some glimmers of hope, and from a surprising source—the Presidency. President Hayes was an honest man who had had nothing to do with the wheeling and dealing that put him in office. He was interested in reforming the government—in particular, the way that jobs were filled in the executive branch. He disliked the use of political patronage by members of Congress to staff such agencies as the Post Office and the various Collectors of Customs; the country was getting political hacks, not the best people, for vital government jobs. Hayes favored a new system for hiring people to work for the federal government—*civil service*. In a civil service system, candidates for government jobs take examinations that measure whether they are qualified for the jobs they seek. Only those people who are most qualified get government jobs.

The Grant Administration had begun some feeble, tentative experiments with civil service, but Hayes was more enthusiastic about the issue. His push for civil service reform angered powerful Republican politicians, such as New York's Senator Roscoe Conkling, who with his cronies used government jobs to reward friends and punish enemies. They still believed in the *spoils system* (to the victors—in war and in politics—belong the spoils) made notorious a half-century before under President Andrew Jackson. Conkling and other Senators saw Hayes's program as a direct threat to their political power. Hayes managed to persuade Congress to enact a limited civil service bill, but Conkling skillfully cut back on its reach.

Conkling's victory turned to ashes during the next Presidential term—1881–1885. Hayes was out of the running for the Republican nomination. After a failed effort by the bosses to get the convention to nominate a willing former President Grant, just back from China, for an unprecedented third term, the leading contenders for the nomination were Blaine and Conkling. These men were leaders of the *Stalwart* faction of Republicans—loyal party members who did not approve of such newfangled ideas as civil service reform. Blaine and Conkling battled to a standstill. In desperation, the delegates seized on handsome, popular James A. Garfield of Ohio. Garfield, who has been thus far the last successful Presidential candidate to emerge from the House of Representatives, was a former chairman of the new and powerful House Appropriations Committee. He had made his reputation by leading an attempt to bring system and honesty to the process of writing and passing bills to finance the government. A brilliant orator, he was the candidate of the reform, or *Mugwump*, faction. (It is uncertain where the word *Mugwump* came from. Some say that it was a Native American word meaning "great chief." Others claim that a Mugwump was someone who wants to be on both sides of an issue; his "mug" is on one side of the fence and his "wump" is on the other side.)

Garfield, an indecisive, timid man, was easily intimidated by Blaine and Conkling. The two great Republican power-brokers forced the nominee to accept a Stalwart, the fashionable Chester A. Arthur of New York, as his running mate. Garfield defeated the Democratic candidate, General Winfield S. Hancock, but found no joy in his victory. He was pulled back and forth over government appointments between Blaine, his new Secretary of State, and Senator Conkling.

At this time, the Senate was evenly divided between Democrats and Republicans, with two independent Senators holding the balance. The Republicans, led by Conkling, managed to persuade one of the independents to vote with them to break the deadlock in order to confirm the President's appointees. But Garfield selected advisers from among the ranks of the Republican Senators, reducing his party's strength in the Senate. Seeing an opportunity to keep control of the Senate, the Democrats tried a "squeeze play." Garfield, too, saw a chance to try to assert himself. He refused to accept Senator Conkling's candidate for the office of Collector of Customs of the Port of New York, the post that Vice President Arthur had held before the election. Conkling and his New York colleague, Thomas Platt, resigned in a dramatic move in May 1881. They claimed that the President had violated the old and honorable tradition of "Senatorial courtesy"—the practice of consulting a state's Senators in appointing federal officials serving in that state. Conkling and

Platt confidently expected to be returned to office, but the New York legislature had other ideas. As they debated the issue of re-electing Conkling and Platt, other events intervened.

Five months after he took office, the President wanted to take a brief vacation. Walking with Secretary Blaine through the waiting room of a Washington, D.C., railroad station, Garfield was shot twice in the back at point-blank range. His assassin, Charles J. Guiteau, was a deranged man who had long sought a government job. Guiteau surrendered himself to police at the scene, grandly declaring, "I am a Stalwart and Arthur is President!" Guiteau had acted on his own, but the incident disgraced the Stalwarts in American politics. Worse tidings for that faction were just over the horizon.

When Garfield died two months later, in terrible pain, one of the Vice President's friends exclaimed, "Chet Arthur President? My God!" Conkling expected to be able to rule the new President, who owed his entire career to him. But Conkling suffered a terrible shock. President Arthur was a new man—almost unrecognizable to those who had known him in New York City as the easy-going Collector of Customs. He adopted civil service as his personal cause and fought to extend President Hayes's reforms to cover many more government jobs in the executive branch. Like Hayes, Arthur was not given his party's nomination for a second term, but he could take comfort that he had achieved his goals.

Arthur's successor, another New Yorker, Grover Cleveland, was the first Democratic President since the disgraced James Buchanan had left office in 1861. Cleveland quickly tangled with Congress over the "private bills" that members of Congress introduced to award government pensions to Civil War veterans and their families. Such private bills usually got speedy treatment from Congress, and previous Presidents had signed them as a matter of course. But Cleveland suspected that most private pension bills were frauds on the public, and he read each one carefully. He vetoed one bill on the grounds that the deceased veteran died from drowning when his buggy overturned in a stream; his widow had claimed that an obscure war injury had been the cause of the fatal accident. A second bill fell to Cleveland's veto because the applicant had served in the Army for only three days in March 1865 without seeing action except for a bout with the measles; the applicant had sought a pension fifteen years later because his "war measles" supposedly had affected his vision and had settled in his spinal column. Most of the nearly six hundred vetoes that Cleveland racked up in his eight years as Chief Executive rejected these private pension bills, and often the President explained his reasons for vetoing the bills with stinging sarcasm. More important, he made the vetoes stick.

In the 1880s and 1890s, the nation was troubled by two major economic issues. Republicans favored tariffs, or taxes on imports, to protect American manufacturers; Democrats argued for free (that is, unrestricted) trade, forcing American businesses to compete with those overseas for the domestic market. The other issue had to do with the nation's currency system. Midwestern and Western farmers facing ruin from debts they owed to Eastern financial interests wanted a way to pay off these debts easily. They wanted the government to inflate the currency and advocated issuing sixteen silver dollars for every gold-backed dollar in circulation. "Gold Democrats" and Republicans opposed the farmers' demands for "free silver," fearing that such inflation would destroy the economy. Congress wrestled with the currency issue throughout the last years of the nineteenth century, repeatedly rejecting the free silver cure-all endorsed by such Democrats as William Jennings Bryan, the perennial Democratic Presidential candidate.

Meanwhile, veteran legislators worried about the growing chaos in the House. The rapidly growing number of standing committees created a set of petty empires, with each committee chairman his own petty emperor. The chairmen often squabbled with one another about who would bring a given piece of legislation to the floor. The resulting disputes strangled the House's methods of doing business. Speaker Samuel J. Randall (Democrat–Maine) tried to focus the process of bringing bills to the floor by giving increased authority to the Rules Committee, but he had only modest success. Other problems facing the House included the members' use of motions for adjournments and quorum calls (both of which required full roll-call votes) and their practice of leaving the floor to deprive the House of a quorum so that it could not do business. These practices abused the rules of the House to delay the process of debating and passing bills. Only a strong Speaker could restrain these abuses and do something to reform the House. Just such a man was on the horizon.

In 1889, the Republican majority in the House elected a new Speaker, Thomas B. Reed of Maine. Reed soon won the nickname "Czar" Reed (after the absolute ruler of Russia) for his vigorous use of his office's authority to reform the House. He announced that he would no longer recognize motions that he deemed "dilatory" or time-wasting. He also announced that he would not tolerate members' attempts to shut down the House by depriving it of a quorum. The test came in a dispute over the election of a Representative from West Virginia. The House vote was 161 Republicans to 5 Democrats, with another 165 Democrats abstaining from voting although they were on the floor of the House. Reed commanded the Clerk to call the roll *and* to record the present but nonvoting Representatives as present, no matter what they said. One Democrat shouted, "I deny your right, Mr. Speaker, to count me as present." Reed replied: "The Chair is making a statement of fact that the gentleman from Kentucky is present. Does he deny it?" The debate continued for three days. When some Representatives tried to leave the chamber, the Speaker ordered the doors locked. (This did not stop one Representative, who kicked down a locked door and thereafter was known as "Kicking-Buck" Kilgore.) Reed's tactics prevailed.

Reed took another giant step toward bringing order to the House by rewriting its rules. He had the power to do so because he was the Chairman of the Rules Committee and Speaker at the same time. The Rules Committee already had won the authority to control which committees got which bills. Under the "Reed rules," the committee handling a particular bill could establish the guidelines for the House's consideration of that bill when it arrived on the floor. This enabled "Czar" Reed and his allies, Joseph Cannon of Illinois and William McKinley of Ohio, to control the business of the House. The Democrats fumed at Reed's high-handed tactics but were helpless to oppose them.

Reed ruled with an iron hand, resigning from the House in 1899 only because he opposed the foreign policy (including the Spanish-American War) of an old friend and former colleague, William McKinley, who was now President. Reed's eventual successor, in 1903, was Joseph Cannon, nicknamed "Uncle Joe." Cannon delighted in the tradition of the strong, autocratic Speaker, pushing his authority far beyond even Reed's hopes for the office. For example, Cannon asserted the right to pass on every bill introduced in the House, no matter how essential or petty it was. He appointed every member of every House committee. As his mentor, "Czar" Reed, had done, Cannon kept a tight grasp on the chairmanship of the all-powerful House Rules Committee. But Cannon's day was past, though he did not recognize it. At the dawn of the twentieth century, he was a relic of the Gilded Age. He soon would have to confront a new style of politics and an active revolt against his dominance of the House.

The Senate had adopted methods similar to Reed's and

Cannon's for bringing its business, including the chairman-ships and staffing of its committees, under the strict control of the majority party's leadership. But the "old guard" who ran the Senate in this period, like their counterparts in the House, were about to suffer a bruising confrontation with a new age in American politics.

CHAPTER SEVEN

THE PROGRESSIVE ERA TRANSFORMS CONGRESS

Historians call the period beginning in the 1890s and continuing until the United States entered the First World War in 1917 the Progressive Era. A wide range of political, economic, legal, and social reformers enlisted under the Progressive banner; they wrote and published and campaigned to reform the United States from top to bottom. Relations between management and labor; the quality of foods, drugs, and other consumer goods; conditions of life in urban slums and factories and on farms; the problems of the millions of immigrants; abuses of economic power; and political corruption and inefficiency—all these subjects were grist for the Progressives' mills.

Congress led the list of Progressives' complaints about the national political system, so Congress felt some of the earliest effects of Progressivism. Also, because the Progressives believed that many of the problems they sought to cure were national problems requiring national solutions, Congress had to deal with their demands for answers.

One of the most important goals of the Progressive movement was the adoption of an amendment to the Constitution requiring that Senators be elected by the people directly instead of by state legislatures. The campaign for this amendment to the Constitution finally succeeded in 1913. In large part, its success was due to the exposure of the corruption and inefficiency of the old Senate.

In 1906, two Senators were convicted of accepting bribes to interfere in the work of federal agencies regulating interstate commerce. This scandal outraged journalists and publishers such as William Randolph Hearst. He ordered his newspapers to conduct a full-scale investigation of what he called "The Treason of the Senate." The exposés shocked the nation. For the first time, the American people began to realize how powerful the Senate was in the constitutional system and how fraud, incompetence, and corruption had stained the state legislatures' election of Senators and the Senate's conduct of its business. Many states found themselves unrepresented in the Senate for weeks or even months as their legislators wrangled, wasted time, and even got into fistfights with one another.

In 1912, the House and Senate approved the proposed Seventeenth Amendment providing for direct election of Senators. Senator William Borah (Republican–Idaho) was the Progressives' hero due to his skillful and tactful guiding of the proposed amendment through the Senate. The Amendment was ratified by the states in 1913. This great symbolic victory heralded a new era in the Senate. As Senators were compelled to undergo the fatigue and stress of political campaigns, they also were forced to learn about the interests and needs of the people they were to represent. The Senate thus grew to reflect the condition of the nation and its people.

The House, too, felt the winds of change. In 1909, Republican Representative George W. Norris of Nebraska stepped forward to lead a challenge to Speaker Cannon. Cannon had continued to rule the House with inflexible hostility to any reform legislation and with an eye to preserving his own authority. Norris led a group of like-minded Progressive Republicans who allied themselves with the Democrats seeking to defeat Cannon's bid for another term as Speaker. The move failed, but the vote was extremely close. Cannon narrowly beat back another Progressive attempt to reform the procedures of the House by stripping him of his chairmanship of the Rules Committee and his power to appoint committee chairmen. But the Progressive Republicans saw that time was on their side. On March 17, 1910, Norris tried again. He offered a proposal to revamp the Rules Committee, to permit its members to elect their own chairman, and to bar the Speaker from membership on the committee. Cannon kept the House in session for twenty-nine straight hours, trying to shore up his support for a final confrontation with Norris. But on March 19, when he ruled Norris's motion out of order, the full House stunned the Speaker by overruling his decision. Norris's motion passed, and the Speaker lost his beloved Rules Committee. It was a major victory for Progressivism and a shattering defeat for Cannon.

Slowly the House began to reshape its procedures and methods of doing business. The process quickened in 1911 when the Democrats had control of the House and sought to undo the legacy of "Czar" Reed and "Uncle Joe" Cannon. The House shifted power from the Speaker to the party leadership. The Majority Leader of the House of Representatives became a new power broker, and the power of the Committee on Ways and Means (the House committee that considers tax bills) began to grow as the Rules Committee's wings were trimmed.

In both the House and Senate, the Democratic and Republican parties were divided into Progressive and conservative blocs. In 1912 and 1913, Democrats allied with Republican Progressives to use Congress's power of investigations to probe the power of concentrated wealth in American society. Chaired by Representative Arsène Pujo (Democrat–Louisiana), this special committee called such leading financiers as J. P. Morgan and grilled them about their holdings, their economic and political power, and their control of the American economic system. The Pujo Committee's report aroused national indignation, and the Democrats vowed to make its findings part of their agenda.

Conservatives still sought to frustrate the legislative programs of Presidents Theodore Roosevelt and Woodrow Wilson, but the two Presidents fought back, managing to wrest some of their most cherished reforms from a reluctant Congress. Such bills as the Pure Food and Drug Act of 1906, the Clayton Anti-Trust Act of 1914, and the Federal Reserve Act of 1914 (the fruit of the Pujo Committee's investigations) were the results of a newly aggressive Presidency.

Roosevelt began the process of trying to set the nation's political and legislative agenda, and Wilson built on his work. In fact, in his first term, Wilson maintained close but secret ties with Representative John Nance Garner (Democrat– Texas), who regularly fed the President political gossip and information about his support and opposition in the House. And Wilson became the first President since John Adams to appear before a joint session of Congress.

President Wilson had a firm base to build on for his knowledge of Congress. In 1885, when he was not yet thirty years of age, he had written his Ph.D. dissertation on Congress. Published later that year as *Congressional Government*, Wilson's pathbreaking book introduced its readers to an institution they barely knew and also introduced the nation to a brilliant student of American public affairs. For the most part, the President demonstrated that he still understood Congress and how to work with that body.

President Roosevelt had always had his greatest successes in duels with Congress over foreign policy. President Wilson was not so fortunate. When the First World War broke out in Europe, in 1914, most Americans wanted the United States to stay out of it. In the 1916 Presidential election, Wilson narrowly won a second term with the slogan "He Kept Us Out of War." But he knew that the war in Europe was worsening and that American interests were being endangered. In particular, Germany's indiscriminate use of a new weapon of war, the torpedo-firing submarine, threatened American shipping and American lives. The Germans had agreed to follow strict rules governing the use of submarine warfare, but Wilson worried that they would change their minds.

The President proposed early in 1917, in the last days of his first term, that the United States arm merchant ships traveling to and from Great Britain and France. The bill stalled in the Senate, where several Senators, led by Progressive Republicans William Borah and George W. Norris, conducted a *filibuster* against it until the Senate adjourned. (A filibuster is a long, drawn-out debate in which opponents of a measure keep control of the floor of the Senate—that is, the right to address the body—as long as they can. They make use of the Senate's long tradition of freedom of debate to retain the floor; even one Senator can conduct a filibuster if he can keep talking and if he has friends on the floor who will give him a few minutes to rest every now and then.) Wilson was infuriated by the Senators' filibuster, declaring: "A little group of willful men, representing no opinion but their own, have rendered the government of the United States helpless and corruptible." Senator Norris retorted, quoting Wilson's own book on Congress: "It is the proper duty of a representative to look diligently into every affair of government and to talk much about what he sees."

The President rallied his supporters to make a major change in the Senate's rules governing debate. The Senate adopted a new *cloture rule* under which it can shut off debate if two-thirds of its members vote to adopt a petition, supported by at least sixteen Senators, to end debate.

The filibuster controversy was forgotten on April 2, 1917.

In a dramatic gesture, the President appeared before a joint session of Congress to announce that Germany had resumed unrestricted submarine warfare against American shipping. He asked for a declaration of war, pledging that the United States was not interested in territorial gain or the other spoils of war. The House and Senate debated the measure for four days and voted to declare war by overwhelming majorities. One opponent of the measure was Representative Jeannette Rankin (Republican–Montana), the first woman elected to the House. She was defeated for re-election in 1918.

Democrats and Republicans in Congress joined ranks to support the Wilson Administration's war effort. This bipartisanship had its less fortunate side. Congress adopted, for the first time in over a century, federal laws restricting freedom of speech and press. The Sedition Act of 1918 prohibited speaking or publishing that might endanger the war effort. This law severely damaged civil liberties in the United States and subjected to arrest and exile hundreds of foreign-born Americans and aliens seeking U.S. citizenship.

In 1918, the President destroyed the bipartisanship brought into being by the war—he urged the voters to return a solid Democratic Congress. Republicans were angered by what they saw as the President's violation of the ground rules of wartime politics, and the voters handed the Democratic President a stinging defeat, electing a Republican House and Senate.

On November 11, 1918, the signing of a truce, or *armistice*, brought joyous celebration of the end of the war throughout the world, and politicians turned their minds to the making of the peace. Again, Wilson erred by renouncing bipartisanship. Instead of appointing prominent Republicans to join him in the American peace delegation, he shut them out. Powerful figures such as Republican Henry Cabot Lodge of Massachusetts, chairman of the Senate Foreign Relations Committee, neither forgave nor forgot the snub. And the Midwestern Progressive Republicans who resented the war, such as Borah and Norris, were not inclined to support the President, either.

Wilson's miscalculation looks even greater when we remember that whatever treaty the President helped to negotiate at the Versailles Conference (at the old French royal palace of Versailles, just outside Paris) had to be approved by two-thirds of the Senate. Word of the Treaty of Versailles leaked back to the United States. Disappointed Democrats and vengeful Republicans alike were startled. Wilson apparently had abandoned all but a handful of his idealistic war aims, the "Fourteen Points." He had endorsed the efforts of the other victorious nations (Britain, France, Italy, and Japan) to carve up the old colonial empires of their defeated opponents (Germany and Austria-Hungary) and to inflict harsh and humiliating punishment on the "aggressor nations." Borah, Norris, and other like-minded Midwesterners, whose constituents included large blocs of German-American voters, were not likely to support this treaty. Moreover, Wilson's ultimate dream, an international peace-keeping organization called the League of Nations, terrified several Senators. They asked troubling questions: Would this League respect American independence? Would it become some sort of supergovernment? Could the Senate adopt this treaty under the Constitution?

The Chief Executive returned home, having convinced himself that the treaty was not just the best that he could get but the best treaty ever. He brushed aside the worries of the Senate and challenged it to reject the treaty that, he declared, carried the hopes of the whole world for an end to all wars. Senator Lodge met the challenge. He did not respect Wilson's learning (after all, he had received Harvard's first doctoral degree in political science, in 1876, nearly a decade before Wilson). He was the senior Republican in the Senate and its most respected member. He had managed to win some minor concessions from the President, and when Wilson made a personal appearance before the Senate to present the treaty for its consideration, Lodge had escorted him onto the floor. Now he warned the President that the treaty was not likely to pass—at least not without revisions.

Senator Lodge proposed that the Covenant of the League of Nations (the proposed world organization's founding document) be detached from the treaty. Wilson rejected this idea indignantly. Lodge and other Republicans also proposed four major and more than forty minor revisions and amendments. Democrats and Republican "mild reservationists" beat back most of these, but it was becoming clear that the treaty would fall short of the two-thirds vote needed for adoption.

President Wilson decided to go over the heads of the Senate to the American people. He set out on a twenty-nine-city cross-country speaking tour, traveling by railroad. In the middle of this tour, he had a physical breakdown, and a couple of weeks later, in October 1919, he suffered a severe stroke in the White House. The President was crippled—some said as crippled as his treaty. On November 7, Lodge presented the treaty to the Senate with fourteen "reservations" (usually called the *Lodge Reservations*). The Senate decisively rejected the treaty—the first time in American history that it had refused to ratify a treaty. This rejection was due in part to Wilson's plea from his sickbed to his supporters to reject a watered-down treaty. Five months later, in March 1920, the Senate again voted on the treaty. This time it received a majority but less than the two-thirds vote needed to ratify.

The treaty fight broke the President and reasserted the independence of the Senate. Partly as a result of Wilson's stubbornness, the Democrats lost control of the Presidency in the 1920 election. For the first time in nearly a century, a sitting Senator—the obscure Warren G. Harding of Ohio—was elected to the Presidency. After the bold leaps of the Progressive Era and the stresses and strains of the war years, the nation—and Congress—settled down to what they hoped would be a period of quiet.

CHAPTER EIGHT

FROM BOOM TO BUST

The American humorist Will Rogers once observed that after a period of great political change and controversy, the American people like "to sleep it off for a while." The 1920s were one such period. But the character of the 1920s was shaped by one last Progressive measure.

Many of the Progressives urged social as well as political reform, and one of their favorite targets was "the evils of strong drink." For most of the nineteenth century and well into the twentieth, reformers campaigned against alcohol. Some advocated *temperance*—getting the people to give up or cut down their drinking on their own. Others believed that only *prohibition*—an outright ban on the manufacture and sale of alcoholic beverages—would work. In 1919, Congress proposed to the states the Eighteenth Amendment, which prohibited the manufacture or sale of virtually any kind of hard liquor, wine, or beer. Congress also adopted the Volstead Act, a law designed to put "the noble experiment" of Prohibition into effect. In 1920, with the ratification of the Eighteenth Amendment, the United States went from "wet" to "dry."

Prohibition may have been a noble experiment, but as an experiment it was a dismal failure. Millions of Americans willingly became lawbreakers because they would not give up alcohol. Criminals such as "Scarface" Al Capone founded huge empires on the demand for illegal, or *bootleg,* alcohol. Smugglers brought in whiskey, Scotch, brandy, and other hard liquor from overseas, evading U.S. Coast Guard patrols. Other enterprising criminals learned to make their own liquor, distilling such beverages as "bathtub gin." Homemade liquor was often dangerous to drink because its manufacturers were not particular about the ingredients they used to make their products. Illegal bars and clubs, called *speakeasies,* flourished throughout the United States. The government could not keep up with those who were willing to violate the law, and many authorities turned a blind eye—for a price. Instead of increasing the virtue of the American people, Prohibition made us a nation of lawbreakers.

The First World War had focused the nation's politics in Washington, D.C., and Congress discovered that its old methods of doing business were inadequate to the new century. The Senate reorganized itself, cutting down on the number of its committees to promote efficiency in dealing with proposed bills. Congress and President Harding also worked together to rethink the way that the budget of the United States should be drawn up. (A *budget* is an itemized list of the sources and amounts of money the government expects to receive, and the ways and amounts that the government expects to spend.) In earlier years, each institution and government agency would submit its own budget request to Congress, which would pass these bills piecemeal. Congress passed and President Harding signed the Budget and Accounting Act of 1921. For the first time in American history, the President was to submit a *unified* budget—a single proposal covering all parts of the government and all sources of revenue. To help him, Congress created the Bureau of the

Budget. The House also decided that all bills for spending money should be handled by one committee, the Appropriations Committee, to avoid wasting time and to give Congress a full picture of how the government was spending its money.

As the 1920s began, the Republican majorities in the House and Senate largely carried on business as usual, and the passive President Harding followed their lead. Harding's Administration included some first-rate officials, but at least as many were mediocre or incompetent, and some were outright crooks. One of the crooks was Senator Albert B. Fall of New Mexico, a clever, grasping man whom Harding named to head the Department of the Interior. Fall used his position to launch what became one of the most famous corrupt deals in American history.

The Navy Department had charge of vast oil fields, called oil reserves, in the Western states. These oil reserves were insurance that the U.S. Navy would have reliable supplies of fuel to power its ships. No one could drill on these oil reserves without a license from the government. Secretary Fall persuaded his dimwitted colleague, Navy Secretary Edwin Denby, to transfer control of the oil reserves to the Interior Department. Then Fall cheerfully pocketed bribes from oil companies in exchange for licenses to drill on the oil reserves. The two reserves at the heart of the scandal were Elk Hills, Nevada, and Teapot Dome, Wyoming.

The Teapot Dome affair was only the most blatant of the many scandals that plagued the Harding Administration. The President was personally honest but had made the mistake of trusting the wrong people. The strain of realizing just how serious a problem he faced was too much for him.

After Harding's sudden death in California in 1923, the signs of corruption were too obvious to ignore. Senator Robert LaFollette, a Wisconsin Republican and leader of that party's dwindling Progressive wing, urged his friend and colleague Democrat Thomas Walsh of Montana to conduct an investigation. Walsh was a former prosecutor who knew how to uncover evidence of wrongdoing. He pressed his investigation, indifferent to the avalanche of public criticism. At first, most Americans believed that the Democrats were just looking for an issue to use against the Republicans in the 1924 Presidential election. But Walsh uncovered too much evidence that the Teapot Dome scandal was real and serious. At the same time, the other Montana Senator, Democrat Burton K. Wheeler, launched his own investigation. His target was Attorney General Harry M. Daugherty, who was taking bribes in return for refusing to enforce the Volstead Act against bootleggers. Fall and Daugherty were forced to resign. Fall became the first Cabinet member to go to prison; Daugherty escaped a jail term by pleading ill health. The Teapot Dome investigations ultimately led to two Supreme Court decisions upholding the power of Congress to conduct investigations and to require witnesses to appear before it. These cases confirmed the continuing importance of Congressional investigations in informing the nation about problems of government and society.

Congress itself was not immune from charges of corruption and wrongdoing. The Senate conducted investigations of several of its own members whose election campaigns were marred by excessive spending and, in some cases, corruption. These charges, and the Harding Administration scandals, led to enactment of the Federal Corrupt Practices Act of 1925. This law was a step in the right direction but in later years proved to be a "toothless tiger."

The nation in the 1920s seemed to be experiencing a remarkable period of growth and prosperity—what stockbrokers called a "boom." But not everyone felt that things were booming. Labor unions had to fight for their very existence against strong-arm tactics by industrialists such as Henry Ford. Farmers were hard-pressed to meet mortgage payments on their farms and equipment. Veterans of the First World War had to lobby Congress persistently for payment of the "bonus" promised them when they were mustered out of the armed forces. For the most part, Congress and the Republican Presidents of the 1920s—Harding and Calvin Coolidge—did little about such problems, and Congress followed their lead.

As Presidents Harding and Coolidge followed a policy of passive leadership and Congress was preoccupied with its own concerns, worried economists noted a growing instability in the American economy. Thousands and thousands of ordinary Americans—retirees, schoolteachers, salesmen, and so forth—were plunging recklessly into the stock market, seeking to make huge profits. At first, they did. At that time, one could call a stockbroker and buy a large quantity of stock *on margin*—by putting up only a small part of the stock's value. Then the investor would wait for the right time to sell, collect the (increased) purchase price, and pay the broker the balance of the original sum he or she had promised to pay for the stock in the first place. Meanwhile, the company paid out part of its profits (in *dividends*) to its stockholders, and everyone was happy. Eager would-be investors plunged themselves into debt to brokerage houses for tens of thousands, or even hundreds of thousands, of dollars. The leading figures in the economic world did the same, on a much larger scale.

Could this ballooning stock market last? If the market finally went "bust," what effect would this have on the economy as a whole? Although many economists began to ask these questions more and more pointedly, no leading political figures ever did. President Coolidge saw no reason to advise caution, and his successor in 1929, the widely respected Herbert Hoover, confidently declared that the United States was about to win the final battle against poverty.

Four dismal weeks in October 1929 changed all that. The bottom fell out of the market, plunging the New York Stock Exchange into panic. Billions of dollars of "paper value" vanished into thin air. The crash at first seemed to have little effect beyond shattering the dreams and careers of the unlucky speculators who had not unloaded their holdings in time. But the ripples spread throughout the economy. Corporations depend upon their stock's value in all sorts of ways. They can borrow money to finance expanding or revamping their facilities and issue new shares of stock to raise new money, or capital, to finance new ventures and explore new markets. If a corporation's stock plunges in value, these dreams dissolve. If the plunge persists, corporations are forced to tighten their belts—to close plants, to fire or lay off workers, to cut other expenses and costs to the bone. These measures cost people their jobs through no fault of their own.

Another way that the effects of the crash were felt throughout the American economy was through the banking system. People deposit money in banks to keep it safe and to earn income—*interest*—from their savings deposits. Banks do not keep this money lying about. They invest it in stocks, bonds, and other enterprises to produce income; they pay out some of this income as interest to their depositors and keep the rest as their profit. Banks suffered losses due to the crash. More important, investors who were wiped out by the crash ran to their savings accounts for money to pay off their debts. So did workers and others who lost their jobs. When all of a bank's depositors converged on that bank at once, the bank could not meet all their demands to withdraw their deposits because they did not have the funds on hand (they were invested elsewhere). Banks failed throughout the nation, leaving millions of Americans without savings.

In this period of American history, people believed that you were on your own in the economy. It was not government's job to help people who lost their jobs or their life's savings or their homes. Secretary of the Treasury Andrew Mellon summed up this view: "Let the slump liquidate itself. Liquidate labor, liquidate stocks, liquidate the farmers. . . . People will work harder, live a more moral life. Values will be adjusted, and enterprising people will pick up the wrecks from less competent people." But the American people's expectations began to change in the years following the 1929 crash— years that are known as the *Great Depression*. Someone had to do something for the millions of jobless, homeless Americans thronging the roads and streets of the United States.

The Hoover Administration was unwilling to take massive action to combat the suffering caused by the Depression. The President and his advisers believed that the United States had no constitutional authority for such measures. Aid to the homeless and the unemployed were matters for state and local governments, if at all. Increasingly the Administration found itself out of step with the people.

In 1931, the Republicans lost control of the House of Representatives. The 1930 congressional elections had cut the Republican margin to one vote, and the deaths of several leading Republicans enabled the Democrats to become the majority party by scoring victories in the special elections to choose replacements. The Senate was also changed by the 1930 elections, with the Republican majority hanging on to control by one vote. For these reasons and because he preferred to deal with the Depression in his own way without the interference of Congress, President Hoover chose not to call a special session of Congress. Thus, Congress did not convene after the 1930 elections until December 1931.

The House chose a new Speaker, Democrat John Nance Garner of Texas, and under his leadership considered and passed emergency measures to deal with the Depression. The Norris-La Guardia Act of 1932, for example, protected labor unions from the most serious abuses of their rights by management. The Senate also proved willing to consider such measures, as conservatives were shouldered aside by their progressive colleagues, Democrats and Republicans alike.

The Senate used its power of investigation to examine the ways in which the nation's financial community, based in

Wall Street in New York City (the home of the New York
Stock Exchange), conducted business. Were there any connections between these business methods and the 1929 crash?
Republican Peter Norbeck of Nebraska, a member of the
progressive group of Republicans, chaired the Senate Banking
Committee investigation of this subject. The committee's
chief counsel, or lawyer, was Ferdinand Pecora. Under Pecora's able and brilliant direction, the committee laid bare
the shortsighted and dangerous abuses in the stock market.
The committee's findings eventually resulted in such major
legislation as the Securities Act of 1933, the Securities Exchange Act of 1934, and the Banking Act of 1933.

These steps, and the publicity given by the Pecora investigations to the need for reforming the nation's financial
system, were not enough to deal with the major crisis that the
Depression posed for the American economy, and even for
the continued survival of constitutional government. The
American electorate demanded change, and in 1932 they got
it. Not only was President Hoover turned out of office by
Democratic nominee Franklin D. Roosevelt (and his running-
mate, Speaker Garner), the Democrats scored overwhelming
victories in the congressional elections as well, winning
control of the Senate and solidifying their hold on the House.

Banks continued to fail throughout 1932 and the early
months of 1933, and the entire nation lived under a cloud of
hopelessness and despair. Rumors abounded of plots by the
military to take over the government. President-elect Roosevelt narrowly escaped assassination in Miami, Florida, in
February 1933. Instead of Hoover's predicted ultimate triumph over poverty, the United States seemed to have reached
rock bottom.

CHAPTER NINE

DEPRESSION AND WAR

Inauguration Day, March 4, 1933, dawned cold and bleak. President Hoover and President-elect Roosevelt rode silently in a limousine to the Capitol building. Hoover was bitter; he had been turned out by the voters in a massive rejection of himself and his policies. He had sought Roosevelt's cooperation in the months between Election Day and Inauguration Day, but the President-elect rebuffed him. Roosevelt did not want his hands tied, nor did he want to be tainted by any alliance with the discredited Hoover Administration.

Roosevelt wasted no time. In his inaugural address, he pledged "action—and action now." He asserted that as President, he had the power and the duty to lead the nation in dealing with the crisis posed by the Depression. He promised to ask Congress for bold measures to combat the Depression's effects on the people. He was as good as his word.

Roosevelt's first step was to proclaim a bank holiday to provide a breathing space for those banks that had not closed their doors. Next, he called Congress into special session to consider emergency legislation. By invoking this power (under Article II, Section 3 of the Constitution), Roosevelt was further distancing himself from his predecessor, who had not seen fit to call a special session of any sort.

When the new Congress gathered in the House and Senate chambers on March 9, they found proposed legislation waiting for them. The first bill, an emergency banking measure, went through the House in thirty-eight minutes flat, with no printed copy of the bill for members to consult. In fact, most members voted for it with a whoop and a roar, not having bothered to read it. The Senate followed suit later in the day, and Roosevelt signed the bill into law that night.

This first bill was followed by many more. The one hundred days that this first session of Congress lasted stand as one of the great periods of cooperation between the President and Congress. In both houses of Congress, the leadership put together steering committees to ensure that laws were considered and passed as quickly as possible in order to give the President and the rest of the Executive Branch the authority and the tools to deal with the Depression. In some instances, the haste to act led to badly drafted and ill-considered laws. At the same time, some of the most lasting achievements of the Roosevelt Administration emerged from the Hundred Days: the Social Security Act, the National Labor Relations Act, and the laws establishing the Federal Deposit Insurance Corporation and the Tennessee Valley Authority. Many of these laws were the handiwork of leading progressive Senators such as George W. Norris and Robert F. Wagner (Democrat–New York).

Shell-shocked at first by the magnitude of their 1932 defeat, Republicans in the House and the Senate reacted to Roosevelt's tornado of legislation in several ways. Some, such as Senators Norris and Arthur Vandenberg of Michigan, worked with the Administration when they felt they could. Others, such as Republican Minority Leader Representative Bertrand Snell of New York and Representative Dewey Short of Missouri, did their best to hold the tide. Short at one point declared that the House was a "supine, subservient, soporific, superfluous, supercilious, pusillanimous body of nitwits." He and his beleaguered colleagues denounced Roosevelt as little short of a dictator, and they raged at their colleagues for following the White House's lead.

In some ways, Snell and Short had a point. During the first years of Roosevelt's Administration, Congress looked to the White House for guidance, direction, and leadership. The President reciprocated; he came more and more to expect that Congress would act on his direction and suggestion. In times of crisis throughout American history, vigorous, activist Presidents have seized the opportunity to place themselves at the focus of events and to lead the government and the nation in dealing with troubles facing the nation. In such times, Congress often follows suit. The question becomes when and how Congress will assert its independence and its right to a voice in the decision-making process.

Roosevelt was buoyed in 1934 by congressional elections that increased the Democrats' control of the House and Senate. And when he ran for a second term, in 1936, he scored one of the most decisive triumphs in the history of American politics, again carrying Congress with him. This extraordinary success had unfortunate consequences, however. The President began to believe that any opposition to his policies could be ignored due to his overwhelming popular mandate.

Alone of the institutions of government at the national level, the Supreme Court was not marching in step with what journalists and government officials alike dubbed the *New Deal*. The Court was dominated by a conservative group of Justices known as "the Four Horsemen of the Apocalypse." The three liberal Justices—Louis D. Brandeis, Benjamin N. Cardozo, and Harlan Fiske Stone—often sat by helplessly as the Four Horsemen carried one or both of the remaining Justices with them. Many of the New Deal measures came

before the Court during Roosevelt's first term, and the Administration suffered a string of major setbacks in the Court. The
worst was the Justices' unanimous rejection of the centerpiece
of the New Deal, the National Industrial Recovery Act. This
law had created an agency called the National Recovery
Administration (NRA), which organized the American economy by industries. Industry councils would have the authority
to write codes for their members; any company violating such
a code would be prosecuted by the NRA. The Justices held
that this law violated the Constitution. Only Congress has
the power to make laws, the Justices declared; Congress may
not *delegate*, or hand over, that power to an executive agency,
and especially not when that agency then delegates that
power to private individuals or corporations.

The President secretly was relieved by the death of the
NRA in 1935, for the agency was not having the effect its
creators had intended or hoped. But he was angered by the
Court's consistent rejection of his New Deal measures. He
consulted with his Attorney General and came up with what
he thought was a brilliant plan to clip the Court's wings.

Roosevelt made a speech to the nation in which he declared
that the "Nine Old Men" of the Court needed help, for they
could not keep up with the Court's business. They could not
retire, for there was no retirement or pension system for
federal judges. Thus, Roosevelt proposed, Congress should
enact a law permitting the President to appoint a new Justice
for each Justice over seventy years of age who chose not to
retire.

Congress received the legislation with doubt and concern.
Its opponents charged that Roosevelt was out to "pack" the
Court with Justices who would vote to uphold New Deal
measures. Even some of the President's supporters were suspi-
cious of the new bill. The Senate Majority Leader, Democrat
Joseph Robinson of Arkansas, demanded Roosevelt's promise

that he would be the first appointee to the Court if he worked to push the bill through the Senate.

The leadership of the House was dubious of the bill. Texas Representative Hatton W. Sumners, chairman of the House Judiciary Committee, drew on his favorite game of poker to explain his reaction: "Boys, here's where I cash in." The President was aware that the House would not look favorably on the measure, so he submitted it to the Senate first, relying on Senator Robinson's skills as Majority Leader. But some of Roosevelt's most loyal allies knew that Robinson had extorted a promise of a Court appointment in return for his support of the bill, and they objected to the idea that this conservative Southern Democrat might wind up on the Supreme Court. Also, many Senators found themselves buried by mail from constituents opposing the measure. The people saw the Court's independence as being part of the Constitution, which in 1937 was 150 years old. They believed that any attempt to damage or cut back the Court's independence would injure the Constitution.

In the midst of the fight over the Court-packing bill, Senator Robinson died. The loss of the chief sponsor of the Court bill doomed the proposal. The Senate sent it back to the Judiciary Committee, burying it forever. The defeat signaled that Congress was no longer willing to jump to the President's commands. It also was a reproof to Roosevelt, who had read too much into his 1936 landslide.

Conservative Southern Democrats joined ranks with Republicans in the Senate to forge a new coalition to oppose the President. In response, still believing that his mandate was a blank check to govern, the President campaigned in the 1938 elections to unseat key members of this coalition, even members of his own party. Roosevelt's efforts to turn the voters against Senators Millard Tydings of Maryland and Walter George of Georgia failed. These Democrats returned to the Senate, determined to wreak vengeance on the President who had trampled party loyalty in his efforts to turn them out of office. The coalition held its ranks, and the President scored few victories on the domestic front thereafter.

Meanwhile, as the President watched developments in Europe and Asia with concern, a feeling of *isolationism* dominated the House and the Senate. *Isolationism* is a shorthand term for the belief that the affairs of Europe, Asia, and Africa are no concern of the United States. Just as the Monroe Doctrine vested primary concern for the affairs of the Western Hemisphere in the hands of the United States, isolationists argued, it meant that the affairs of the Eastern Hemisphere were their own business. They cited the heartbreaking experience of Woodrow Wilson during the negotiations of the Treaty of Versailles nearly two decades earlier. Look, they said, at what happens when we try to tell Europe how to behave.

Thus the isolationists ignored the warning signs in the 1930s: the growing ambitions of the Japanese in the Far East; the rise of dictators Adolf Hitler in Germany and Benito Mussolini in Italy; Mussolini's conquest of the African nation of Ethiopia; Hitler's annexation of Austria and, later, of Czechoslovakia. They suffered a major blow to their cause when Hitler and the Soviet Union invaded Poland on September 1, 1939, touching off the Second World War. As President Roosevelt told the nation, "This nation will remain a neutral nation, but I can not ask that every American remain neutral in thought as well." The United States began some preparations to shore up its military power. (In this campaign, the President had the support of Southern conservatives in the House and Senate—the same people who had opposed his domestic policies.) The first peacetime draft in the nation's history got under way in late 1940. In March 1941, Congress approved Roosevelt's inspired *Lend-Lease program*. The United States would supply the British with fifty over-age destroyers in return for ninety-nine-year leases of British military and naval bases in the Western Hemisphere. Isolationists charged that Roosevelt was scheming to drag the United States into war on the side of Britain and France against Germany, Italy, Japan, and the U.S.S.R., but they were ignored.

Still, the isolationists managed to resist the President's efforts to position the United States as a quiet, informal ally of Britain and France. In large part, they believed that European wars were irrelevant to American interests and needs, and they were confident that the United States was protected from involvement in war by the Atlantic and Pacific oceans. How, they asked, could any power strike a blow at American territory?

The Japanese surprise attack on the U.S. naval base at Pearl Harbor, Hawaii, on December 7, 1941, answered their question. The next day, the President appeared before a stunned Congress meeting in joint session. He read a six-minute address denouncing Japan and demanding a declaration of war. Congress responded with a thunderous ovation. Meeting separately, the House and the Senate swiftly answered his call. One leading isolationist, Republican Senator Arthur Vandenberg of Michigan, repented before his colleagues: "I have fought every trend which I thought would lead to needless war; but when war comes to us—and particularly when it comes like a thug in the night—I stand with my Commander in Chief for the swiftest and most invincible reply of which our total strength may be capable." In the Senate, the vote to declare war against Japan was unanimous. In the House, one lone Representative held out: pacifist Jeannette Rankin, a Montana Republican who had been returned to the House in the 1940 election. Miss Rankin had voted against American entry into the First World War as well; she was the only member of either house of Congress to oppose both wars. (As in 1918, she was defeated for re-election in 1942.)

Both the House and the Senate supported the Administration's measures to prosecute the war, but conservatives were vigilant against any attempt by the Administration to continue the work of the New Deal under the guise of wartime measures. At the same time, Congress tried to monitor government spending on the mammoth war effort. A little-known Senator from Missouri, Democrat Harry S Truman, became chairman of the Senate's Special Committee to Investigate the National Defense Program. Truman was a loyal supporter of Roosevelt (he had even backed the President's ill-fated Court-packing bill in 1937), but he worked vigorously to expose and combat waste in wartime spending. His committee's investigations saved the nation millions of dollars and won the admiration of many Administration officials, including the President. Truman's sole rebuff came when he discovered and tried to investigate a secret government project, the Manhattan Project. High-ranking Administration officials explained to Truman, and to leading members of the House, that this project was vital to the war effort and that it was essential to preserve its secrecy. The Representatives and Senators accepted these explanations.

Truman's work against government wartime waste made him an attractive national candidate in 1944. Roosevelt had already broken the hallowed two-term tradition for Presidents in 1940; because "Cactus Jack" Garner wanted to retire (and because he resisted Roosevelt's bid for a third term), the President had chosen his Secretary of Agriculture, Henry A. Wallace, as his Vice Presidential running mate. But Vice President Wallace proved to be too controversial, especially in his starry-eyed admiration for the U.S.S.R., a new ally of the United States and Great Britain in the war against Hitler and Mussolini. Roosevelt and his aides agreed to "dump" Wallace and selected Truman as his replacement. Thus, in

January 1945, Roosevelt's third Vice President moved from the floor of the Senate, where he had served for nearly ten years, to the presiding officer's chair. He sat there for eighty-three days, writing letters to his family as Senators droned on in debate. On April 12, 1945, as he went to have a drink with his old Senate cronies at the end of the day, Truman received a telephone call from the White House. He rushed to the President's residence, where he learned that Roosevelt had died that day at his health retreat in Warm Springs, Georgia. From a job where the only interesting thing he could do was to write letters, the Missourian had been catapulted into the most powerful office in the United States.

The new President soon discovered the truth about the Manhattan Project from Secretary of War Henry L. Stimson. The government had been working secretly to develop and perfect a weapon using the energy of the atom. Work on this new "atomic bomb" was proceeding satisfactorily, stimulated by fears that Germany was also working to develop such a weapon. Truman discussed his news only with those House and Senate leaders who already had been briefed by the War Department. No leaks emerged from the White House or from Capitol Hill of work on the atomic bomb. Even the first successful test of the weapon—on July 16, 1945, at Trinity Site, Alamogordo, New Mexico—was kept secret. It was not until three months after the suicide of Adolf Hitler and the surrender of Germany (V-E Day) that the nation and the world learned of atomic weapons. The United States exploded their last two over the Japanese cities of Hiroshima and Nagasaki, in August 1945. The nuclear destruction of these two cities led to Japan's abrupt and unconditional surrender (V-J Day). President Truman and Congress celebrated the end of the war and tried to figure out how to deal with the postwar world.

CHAPTER TEN

POSTWAR CRISES AT HOME AND ABROAD

The events of Franklin D. Roosevelt's Presidency—the Great Depression and the New Deal, the Second World War, and the development of the atomic bomb—caused a major shift in the balance of power and authority between Congress and the President. This change manifested itself in several ways:

1. The paralysis of President Hoover and of Congress during the first years of the Great Depression caused the American people to welcome a strong, activist Presidency such as that of Franklin Roosevelt. They came to expect a President to lead, to provide direction, clarity, and foresight about the interests of the nation at home and abroad. The President became the national spokesman, the national civics teacher, and the national source of American policy. Congress more and more found itself reacting to Presidential initiative, providing leadership of its own only when the President could not or would not lead.

2. Although Congress in the past had deferred to the President in matters of foreign policy, it still had retained control over questions of war and peace. As a result of the Second World War, however, the technology of communica-

tion and transportation had revolutionized warfare. The President could receive more information and act on it far more rapidly than Congress could. President Truman unwittingly encouraged this trend in 1947 when he approved the creation of the Central Intelligence Agency. This agency, and its counterpart, the National Security Agency, permitted Truman and his successors to justify foreign-policy decisions by citing access to secret information. Critics of White House policy were answered with the wistful claim "If you knew what we know . . ."

3. The successful development of the atomic bomb gave the President, as Commander-in-Chief of the armed forces, control of a weapon that transformed warfare into a threat to the continued existence of human life. Just as Theodore Roosevelt could boast in 1906 that "I took the [Panama] Canal and let Congress debate," a modern President could launch a nuclear war by himself, with no time for Congress to debate. As a result, Congress deferred to an official possessing the power to end life on the planet.

4. Finally, the sudden emergence of the Soviet Union as the principal rival of the United States and the "leader of world Communism" terrified Congress, just as much as it alarmed President Truman and the American people. The U.S.S.R. had eventually allied itself with the United States during the Second World War. Most Americans conveniently forgot that the Soviet leader, Chairman Joseph Stalin, had allied the U.S.S.R. with Germany, Italy, and Japan in the opening years of the war. At the war's end, the U.S.S.R. refused to withdraw its forces from the nations of Eastern Europe, imposed Communist-dominated governments on most of those countries, and annexed others (such as Estonia, Latvia, and Lithuania) outright. Former British Prime Minister Winston S. Churchill, in a 1946 speech at Westminster College, in Fulton, Missouri, described the Soviet Union as having lowered "an iron curtain" across Europe. The

U.S.S.R. had also developed atomic weapons—a development that representatives of the U.S. armed forces had assured the nation was impossible for decades. A few years later, the U.S.S.R. had caught up with the United States in the arms race by developing the hydrogen bomb, the first of a class of thermonuclear weapons far outstripping the power of atomic weapons. The United States and the U.S.S.R. faced each other in an atmosphere of mutual suspicion and hostility barely short of actual armed conflict. Journalists dubbed this tense rivalry the Cold War. The threat of the Soviet Union, whether real or exaggerated, dominated foreign policy for decades and helped to shape Congressional action at home as well.

At first, the end of the Second World War left the United States in a commanding position on the stage of world affairs. President Truman shepherded into existence the United Nations, the late President Roosevelt's dream for an international peacekeeping organization with teeth. Unlike Woodrow Wilson's disastrous experience with the Senate nearly thirty years earlier, President Truman worked closely with Republican leaders in the Senate, such as Arthur Vandenberg, making them partners in the creation of the United Nations and in determining the shape of the postwar world. Vandenberg also became the architect of another international alliance, the North Atlantic Treaty Organization. The Senate approved both the Truman Doctrine in 1947, which authorized postwar economic aid to Greece and Turkey, and the Marshall Plan in 1948, which did the same for war-ravaged Europe.

Truman had little success on the domestic front, however. American voters resented what they saw as the slowness of the nation's return to a peacetime footing. They wanted an end to price and wage controls, an end to shortages and rationing of such items as gasoline, paper, and rubber. In the congressional elections of 1946, the Republicans took back control of both houses of Congress. They systematically frustrated President Truman's attempts to build on the New Deal legacy of President Roosevelt.

The Republican-dominated Congress enacted over a Presidential veto the Taft-Hartley Act of 1947, a significant law governing labor-management relations. Management cheered the adoption of Taft-Hartley, which they thought evened the balance between management and labor that the National Labor Relations Act had tilted in labor's favor. Labor naturally resented the new law, which permitted many states (mostly in the South and Midwest) to adopt *right-to-work laws* forbidding management to make membership in a labor union a condition of employment. Senator Robert A. Taft of Ohio, the architect of the Taft-Hartley Act, became the leading candidate of conservative Republicans for the 1948 Presidential nomination.

The Democrats made it a priority to regain control of Congress in the 1948 elections, although many party leaders feared that the Democrats would face disaster unless they dumped President Truman. Truman refused to be dumped, however. He won nomination for a term of his own, but the Southern wing of his party walked out of the Democratic National Convention in anger over the party's adoption of a strong civil-rights plank in its platform. The "progressive" wing also walked out, declaring its opposition to the Truman Administration's Cold War policy of confrontation toward the Soviet Union. The President rallied the remaining Democrats at their listless convention. He tore into the "do-nothing Eightieth [Republican] Congress" and announced that he was calling Congress back into session to deal with his domestic agenda. He spent the rest of the campaign traveling 31,700 miles around the nation by train, lambasting the "do-nothing" Congress at every whistlestop, making 356 speeches in all. At the same time, the Democratic strategists picked able, talented, and committed liberal candidates to lead their effort to retake Congress from the Republicans. Both campaigns worked. Truman surprised journalists, pollsters, and political experts throughout the country by scoring a narrow but decisive victory over Republican Governor Thomas E. Dewey of New York, and the Democratic "class of 1948" handed Congress back to the Democrats. The freshmen Democratic Senators who took office in 1949 included such later titans as Lyndon B. Johnson of Texas, Hubert H. Humphrey of Minnesota, Paul Douglas of Illinois, Russell Long of Louisiana, and Estes Kefauver of Tennessee. Also a member of the "class of 1948," but a Republican, was Margaret Chase Smith of Maine, the first woman to be elected to the Senate without having first succeeded her husband. (Governors usually appointed the widow of a deceased Senator to serve out his term.)

The Democrats' triumph was short-lived, however. The Republicans capitalized on American fears of the U.S.S.R. in the Cold War and mounted a series of sensational congressional investigations in the House and the Senate. The House Un-American Activities Committee, which had been launched in the late 1930s to investigate Nazi and Communist movements in the country, focused its attention on the American Communist Party and on other organizations affiliated with, supported by, or sometimes simply agreeing with the Communists. One member of the Committee was a young Republican from California, Richard M. Nixon. Nixon's shrewd understanding of the Communist issue and his gift for investigation led him to Whittaker Chambers, an editor of *Time* magazine, who disclosed that he had been a member of the Communist Party and that he had engaged in espionage for the Soviet Union during the 1930s and early 1940s with the help of a State Department official named Alger Hiss. Hiss, a highly respected member of the liberal "establishment," confronted Chambers at a well-publicized session of the Committee; he challenged Chambers's story and accused him of *perjury* (lying under oath). But Nixon and his aides believed Chambers and managed to uncover sufficient evidence to cast at least some doubt on Hiss's story. Thus, it was Hiss—not Chambers—who was indicted for perjury and eventually convicted and imprisoned. Nixon's sharp questioning of Hiss during the Committee session, and his relentless digging for evidence to rehabilitate Chambers, attracted national attention. He later built on the Hiss-Chambers case to score a surprise victory in his 1950 bid to represent California in the Senate.

One Republican Senator who learned from Nixon's success with the Communist issue was Joseph McCarthy of Wisconsin. McCarthy was floundering in his career in the late 1940s, seeking a headline-making issue to keep himself afloat. In several widely publicized speeches in 1950, McCarthy charged that anywhere from 81 to 205 members of the Truman Administration were known Communists and active agents of the Soviet Union. Democratic Senator Millard Tydings of Maryland convened a hearing of a special panel of the Senate Foreign Relations Committee to hear McCarthy's charges. The committee rejected McCarthy's claims as unfounded and condemned the Senator for foisting "a fraud and a hoax" on the American people. But McCarthy bounced back, denouncing Tydings as a dupe of the international Communist conspiracy. That autumn, Tydings, who had survived President Franklin D. Roosevelt's attempts to drive him from office in 1938, was defeated—in large part by anti-Communist hysteria fomented by McCarthy and his allies.

Tydings was not the only victim of McCarthy's venom. When Republican Senator William Benton of Connecticut introduced a resolution in 1951 calling for his fellow Republican McCarthy's expulsion from the Senate, McCarthy replied: "Benton has established himself as a hero of every Communist and crook in and out of government." Benton lost his seat in the 1952 Senate elections, an unusual case in an election in which the Republicans won back the Senate. McCarthy claimed credit for Benton's defeat.

Tydings and Benton were merely the most notable victims of the Senator from Wisconsin. McCarthy and his counter-parts on the House Un-American Activities Committee (HUAC) also helped to destroy the lives and careers of dozens of men and women in all walks of life. Unsupported accusations, followed by subpoenas commanding them to testify before either McCarthy's Permanent Subcommittee on Investigations of the Senate Government Operations Committee or the HUAC, left witnesses squirming under newsreel and television cameras as hostile questioners berated them for refusing to disclose information about their past lives. Some witnesses declared that they had a right under the First Amendment's guarantee of freedom of association not to disclose their past associations with Communist organizations or other organizations on various "subversive" lists. The committees rejected these claims, and they were backed up by the courts. Other witnesses invoked their right not to say anything that might be used against them, a right protected by the Fifth Amendment—but this tactic led to the term *Fifth Amendment Communist* and the unjustifiable suspicion in the minds of Congress and the general public that anyone invoking the Fifth Amendment must have something to hide. A new and ugly word entered the American language—*McCarthyism*, the use of unsupported charges and smear tactics to destroy someone's reputation and career.

Many journalists gave up in frustration trying to pin Senator McCarthy down. The Senator would make a host of charges, like a squid squirting ink, and while the press tried to sort out the facts to find out if the charges had substance, he would jet off in another direction, shooting off more charges. The exasperation of some of McCarthy's colleagues grew to the breaking point. Three Democratic members of his committee resigned in protest at his tactics. When he offered to make some changes in his procedures, they returned, only to be offended again as McCarthy resumed his usual methods.

One reason for McCarthy's success was that his anti-Communist campaign coincided with the beginning of American military involvement in Korea. In June 1950, North Korea had invaded South Korea. The United Nations voted to condemn the action and to send an international peacekeeping force to the beleaguered peninsula. President Truman, invoking his authority as Commander-in-Chief, committed American soldiers to ground combat in Korea as part of the U.N. effort. Although he did not ask Congress for a declaration of war, there was little if any resistance to Truman's decision. It was thus hard to challenge McCarthy's campaigns against alleged Communist conspiracies at home when American soldiers were being killed resisting Communist aggression abroad.

Many observers believed that McCarthy's reign of terror was designed to propel the Republican Party into the Presidency. With the election of Dwight Eisenhower in 1952, they hoped, the Senator would cease and desist. But McCarthy only stepped up his attacks. President Eisenhower was disgusted but did not reprove McCarthy. In early 1954, McCarthy overreached himself: He took on the U.S. Army, launching investigations into Army decisions to promote servicemen with alleged Communist connections and sympathies. But the Army was not like McCarthy's earlier targets. Secretary of the Army Robert Stevens demanded a chance to confront the Senator and answer his charges. The Army appointed noted Boston attorney Joseph Welch as its counsel. McCarthy and Welch tangled repeatedly from April through June 1954, as the nation watched on television. The American people finally had an in-depth exposure to the Senator's tactics, and they were repelled by what they saw and heard. Joseph Welch became an instant American hero for his insistence on fairness and his unfailing courtesy and willingness to abide by

U.S. Senate

Senator Joseph R. McCarthy (Republican–Wisconsin), a symbol of the abuse of Congress's power to investigate, conducted witch-hunts for Communists and "traitors" in government and public life from 1950 to 1954. McCarthy gestures with a pointer during the 1954 Army-McCarthy hearings; watching him, head in hand, is Joseph Welch, the Army's counsel in those hearings. The confrontation between the Senator and the Army severely damaged McCarthy's credibility and led to his censure by his exasperated colleagues in December 1954.

the rules. McCarthy made a fatal misstep aimed straight at Welch: He charged that a lawyer on Welch's staff was a former Communist. Welch, aghast at McCarthy's breach of ground rules that he had helped to frame, demanded of the Senator, "At long last, have you no sense of decency, sir?" The question reverberated throughout the nation, and within six months the Senate answered.

In December 1954, the Senate voted, sixty-seven to

twenty-two, to *censure,* or condemn, McCarthy. Vice President Nixon, who had supported McCarthy earlier, now worked with the Senate leadership to handle the McCarthy censure as fairly and smoothly as possible. With his censure, McCarthy faded from respectability. The Democrats succeeded in winning back control of the Senate in the 1954 elections, and as a result McCarthy lost his committee chairmanships. His drinking problem got the upper hand, and in May 1957 the junior Senator from Wisconsin died, alone and forgotten. (One of the members of the committee hearing the censure charges was a freshman Democrat from North Carolina, Samuel J. Ervin, Jr. Twenty years later, while chairing a Senate select committee of his own, Ervin would remember his exposure to McCarthy's tactics.)

The McCarthy affair left a bitter taste in the mouths of Senators and Representatives alike. Doubts grew about the usefulness and appropriateness of televised congressional investigations. Senator Estes Kefauver, a freshman Tennessee Democrat, also had catapulted himself into the headlines in 1950 and 1951 with a series of dramatic investigations into organized crime. Kefauver never made unsubstantiated charges, but many of his colleagues wondered whether grilling reluctant witnesses under harsh television lights was anything more than sensational theatre and a way to grab headlines. In 1952, Speaker of the House Sam Rayburn (Democrat–Texas) barred television, radio, and film coverage of all House committee hearings. After McCarthy's censure, both the House and the Senate adopted stricter rules and procedures governing the conduct of committee investigations and preserving the rights of witnesses. In the late 1950s, the Supreme Court also handed down several decisions on Congress's powers over witnesses in its investigations, building on, but refining, its decisions from the 1920s to take more account of individual rights.

In 1954, nearly a century after the last instance of bloodshed in Congress, the nation was stunned by a terrorist attack on the House of Representatives. As the House was conducting a vote in open session, four gunmen opened fire on the floor from the visitors' gallery. As members dove for cover and the Speaker declared the session adjourned, five Representatives fell wounded. A sixth dashed up the stairs to the gallery and overpowered one of the gunmen. The four terrorists were Puerto Rican nationalists. They demanded independence for Puerto Rico, which has been a commonwealth under U.S. authority and protection since the Spanish-American War of 1898. The injured Representatives recovered, and the gunmen were eventually sent to prison.

Republicans lost control of both houses of Congress in 1954. Two Democrats from Texas, one a veteran and the other a relative newcomer, thus moved into leadership positions in the House and Senate.

The quiet, universally respected Sam Rayburn reclaimed the Speakership from Republican Joseph W. Martin of Massachusetts. Rayburn was a different kind of Speaker. He believed in persuasion and reason rather than the force and bluster of earlier Speakers such as "Czar" Reed and "Uncle Joe" Cannon. He held the Speakership more than twice as long as any of his predecessors (1940–1947, 1949–1951, 1955–1961).

No one respected and admired Rayburn more than Lyndon B. Johnson, who had begun his legislative career in the House as a protégé of "Mr. Sam." When Johnson moved over to the Senate in 1948, he kept up his close ties with the Speaker. In 1953, due to the death of Senator Robert A. Taft of Ohio, which gave Democrats a one-vote margin in the Senate, Johnson became the youngest man (at forty-six) ever to hold the office of Senate Majority Leader. Although more forcefully persuasive than Rayburn—Johnson used hardball tactics and the sheer raw power of his personality to woo or intimidate his colleagues—the new Majority Leader refused to make use of the blatant strong-arm tactics of a bygone era. In

*The Democratic leadership of Congress in the late 1950s was a
tough, well-organized, professional team of legislators:
standing, left to right, Senator George Smathers (Florida),
Senator Lyndon B. Johnson (Texas), Senator Hubert H.
Humphrey (Minnesota), Representative John W. McCormack
(Massachusetts), Representative Carl Albert (Oklahoma);
sitting, left to right, Speaker of the House Sam Rayburn (Texas),
Senator Mike Mansfield (Montana).*

addition, he endeared himself to other freshman Senators by
revising the Senate's methods of assignment to committees so
that new Senators had a better chance of assignment to
important ones such as the Foreign Relations or Judiciary
Committees rather than having to serve in limbo on such
bodies as the Committee on the Post Office. Johnson held
this post from 1953 to 1961, when he became Vice President.

Rayburn and Johnson deferred to President Eisenhower in
the fields of foreign policy and defense, but in one case, in

1954, they resisted a Presidential initiative. The French were facing defeat in their efforts to suppress a Communist-led independence movement in Vietnam, part of the dwindling French colonial empire. The President was ready to send American airplanes to provide air cover for the French forces besieged in the city of Dienbienphu. Johnson and Rayburn declared their opposition to the proposed measure and managed to avert it. (Johnson's part in this incident is especially ironic in light of American involvement in the Vietnam quagmire during his Presidency a decade later.)

In 1957, the Soviet Union shocked the United States by launching Sputnik I, the first man-made satellite, into Earth orbit. A few months later, the American space program suffered two embarrassing failures to get its first satellite into space. Senator Johnson made space his issue. He challenged the Eisenhower Administration's mild reaction to the Soviet achievement and urged in Congress and in the news media that the United States mount a vigorous space program. Johnson succeeded in his aim. The incident is significant because it shows how Congress can assume initiative in a given area of national policy if—but only if—a President cannot or will not provide that leadership.

Johnson also assumed leadership of the move to enact a civil rights bill in 1957—an ironic role for a Southerner. Virtually every Southern Democratic Senator had opposed civil rights measures since President Truman had attempted to secure the first a decade earlier. The quest for federal protection for civil rights had helped to divide the Democratic Party in 1948, and Southern Senators grew skilled in their use of Senate rules and tactics, such as the filibuster, to block enactment of such measures. It took the wiliness and brilliant political instincts of Lyndon Johnson to ram the 1957 bill through a reluctant Senate. Johnson demonstrated that he had the skills and the commitment to effect policy in the national interest. He became a leading contender for the 1960 Democratic Presidential nomination.

The last two years of the Eisenhower Administration witnessed major changes in Congress. The Democrats solidified their majorities in the House and Senate, and Congress clashed repeatedly with an increasingly conservative President. Both parties were positioning themselves for the 1960 Presidential election.

In the narrowest Presidential election since 1916, the Democrats captured the White House. The victorious candidate was Senator John F. Kennedy of Massachusetts. Not only was Kennedy the youngest man elected to the Presidency, and the first Catholic President, he was the first Senator to win the Presidency since Warren G. Harding in 1920. He had defeated Johnson for the nomination but chose the Texan as his running mate to demonstrate that the party had national support and appeal. The Kennedy-Johnson ticket edged the Republicans' nominees, Vice President Nixon and Henry Cabot Lodge (the son of the Massachusetts Senator who had led opposition to the Treaty of Versailles in 1919).

With the transfer of power from the Eisenhower to the Kennedy Administration, the United States and Congress moved out of the postwar era. The next few years would complete the transition from a generation of politicians molded by the New Deal to a new generation of politicians more skeptical of tradition and deference and more willing to shake things up in order to get things done.

CHAPTER ELEVEN

FROM THE NEW FRONTIER TO WATERGATE

In 1961, the year in which President Kennedy's Administration took office under the slogan "The New Frontier," the character of Senate leadership changed once again. The Democratic majority elected the gentle, soft-spoken Mike Mansfield of Montana its new Majority Leader. Mansfield's scholarly, low-key style was an abrupt change from the expansiveness of Lyndon Johnson. Some Democrats criticized Mansfield as being too weak, too willing to let Senators go their own way. Mansfield retorted that the traditions of the Senate encouraged its members to be independent; he was not going to try to steamroll his colleagues. But under Mansfield's tenure as Majority Leader, the divisions of the Democratic majority into liberals, moderates, and Southern conservatives grew.

The House, too, witnessed its share of difficulties. In his last great battle, Speaker Rayburn challenged the House Rules Committee. The committee's chairman, Representative Howard "Judge" Smith of Virginia, had used the committee's power over the agenda of the House to bottle up legislation that he opposed. Liberals were exasperated by his tactics and in the late 1950s tried to challenge Smith or to break the power of the Rules Committee. Speaker Rayburn headed them off, promising that in the next Congress he would ensure that the committee would no longer act as an obstacle to the work of the House.

The lines were drawn in January 1961. A new Democratic President was relying on the old Speaker (Rayburn was nearly twice Kennedy's age). Rayburn and Smith dueled for weeks in a now-legendary battle over rules, committee size and membership, and votes. Rayburn's goal was to increase the size of the committee; Rayburn would appoint enough liberal Democrats to break the Southern conservatives' hold on the agenda of the House. Republicans cheered on the conservative Democratic chairman. One journalist reported that pressures on both sides were so high that one Representative changed his mind six times during the course of the contest. During the last roll call vote, the House and the galleries held their collective breath waiting for the tally. By a vote of 217–212, Rayburn prevailed. His defeat of "Judge" Smith was his last major triumph; he died of cancer in November of that year. Rayburn's victory did not solve all of the Administration's problems, for Smith was still chairman of the committee, but his power had been weakened significantly.

The early 1960s were frustrating years for the Kennedy Administration because the President had little success in getting his domestic agenda through Congress. As a result, the President became more and more interested in foreign affairs, where Congress generally deferred to Presidential leadership. The Kennedy Administration never made effective use of its most able and experienced expert on Congress— Vice President Johnson, who languished in frustration and boredom, aching to be consulted. It is still not clear why Kennedy never called on the services of his Vice President, although many observers of the Kennedy-Johnson relationship have cited the mutual distrust between the Vice President and Attorney General Robert F. Kennedy, the President's brother and closest adviser.

During the 1960 campaign, John Kennedy had chided his predecessor, Dwight Eisenhower, for his failure to provide vigorous executive leadership. In 1962, a chastened and reflective President Kennedy met three network news correspondents for a televised conversation about his Presidency and mused that Congress looked different from his end of Pennsylvania Avenue from the way he had seen it when he was in the Senate in the late 1950s.

As the friendly, anti-Communist government of South Vietnam came under increasing pressure from the Communist government of North Vietnam and from a pro-Communist local resistance movement (the Vietcong), President Kennedy decided to continue to honor the Eisenhower Administration's commitment to South Vietnam and to expand American involvement in that conflict. Congress again backed up the President in a foreign policy initiative. It was the beginning of a massive American commitment that would tear the nation apart before the end of the decade.

With Kennedy's assassination on November 22, 1963, Lyndon Johnson became President. The new Chief Executive appeared before a joint session of Congress and declared, "All I have I would gladly give not to be standing here today. . . . Let us continue." At last Johnson was in a position to use his unsurpassed political skills to push a legislative program through Congress. He repeatedly invoked the murdered Kennedy and reminded the gasping members of the House and Senate, "I'm the only President you've got." Within a year, he had rammed through a legislative agenda, including new and stronger civil rights bills, that Kennedy had tried without success to get enacted. Congress meekly followed the President's lead.

President Johnson confronted the growing American involvement in Vietnam in the summer of 1964. Reports of a clash in international waters off the coast of North Vietnam between an American destroyer and North Vietnamese patrol boats induced Congress to adopt the *Tonkin Gulf Resolution.* It permitted the President "to take all necessary measures to repel any armed attack against the forces of the United States and to prevent further aggression . . . [and] to take all necessary steps, including the use of armed force, to assist any member or protocol state of the Southeast Asia Collective Defense Treaty requesting assistance in defense of its freedom." The House adopted the resolution by a vote of 416–0; the Senate adopted it by a vote of 88–2. President Johnson repeatedly invoked this resolution as the equivalent of a declaration of war authorizing American military involvement in Vietnam.

Congressional opposition to the Vietnam conflict grew, however, as the 1960s dragged on with little sign that the war was accomplishing anything in support of democracy or defense of America's allies. Senators Wayne Morse (Republican–Oregon) and J. William Fulbright (Democrat–Arkansas) took the floor to speak out against the war, and Fulbright's Senate Foreign Relations Committee held televised hearings that cast doubt on the war's aims, legality, and eventual success. Two Democratic Senators—Eugene McCarthy (Minnesota) and Robert F. Kennedy (New York), the former Attorney General—each challenged Johnson for the 1968 Democratic Presidential nomination. When Johnson (realizing that he would lose his bid for renomination) withdrew from the campaign in March 1968, Vice President Hubert H. Humphrey of Minnesota became the Administration's candidate. In a bitter, divisive year that witnessed the assassination of Senator Kennedy on the night of his victory in the California primary and the murder in Memphis, Tennessee, of the Nobel Peace Prize-winning civil rights leader Reverend Martin Luther King, Jr., the Presidential election resulted in a narrow victory for former Vice President Richard M. Nixon, the

Republican nominee. Nixon's victory did not manage to break the Democrats' control of either the House or the Senate, however.

Congress dealt in these years with outcroppings of corruption among its members. The former secretary to Lyndon Johnson when he was Majority Leader, Bobby Baker, was indicted and convicted for tax fraud and other violations of the federal corrupt practices laws. Democratic Senator Thomas F. Dodd of Connecticut was censured by his colleagues for conduct "which is contrary to accepted morals, derogates from the public trust expected of a Senator and tends to bring the Senate into disfavor and disrepute." In 1967, the same year as Dodd's censure, the House voted to oust Democratic Representative Adam Clayton Powell of New York for a variety of offenses. In a special election, Powell's constituents returned him to his seat, sympathizing with his claims that the House had acted against him because he was black. He filed suit in federal court challenging his ouster and again won re-election in 1968. In 1969, the Supreme Court ruled that the House had no power to take Powell's seat away from him; later that year, the House voted to fine him $25,000 and strip him of his *seniority*—the increased status and privileges that go with length of service in Congress. Powell was defeated in a 1970 Democratic primary in his district.

The year 1969 witnessed a rebellion against the power of the Speaker of the House. Frail, old Democrat John McCormack of Massachusetts had succeeded the late Sam Rayburn as Speaker in 1961. An insurgent movement among liberal Democratic members challenged McCormack's bid for re-election as Speaker; the rebels backed Democratic Representative Morris K. Udall of Arizona. Udall was defeated, but McCormack got the message and announced that he would retire from the House at the end of his term. (He was succeeded by Representative Carl Albert of Oklahoma.)

Again, the traditions of the House, like those of the Senate, were under assault by new members who had different ideas about what Congress should be.

President Nixon was not generally popular and disdained working with Congress. As a result, he suffered significant defeats in key items on his agenda. In 1970, he was unable to get two Supreme Court nominees, Clement Haynsworth and then G. Harrold Carswell, confirmed by the Senate. The Carswell defeat, which was unprecedented in the history of the Senate or of the Court, was due largely to the clear contempt for the Senate that Nixon had demonstrated by picking so unqualified a nominee for the Supreme Court. Other legislative initiatives failed as well. In fact, in late 1970, Congress repealed the Tonkin Gulf Resolution. The Senate also adopted a resolution sponsored by Republican John Sherman Cooper of Kentucky and Democrat Frank Church of Idaho restricting the use of American combat forces in Cambodia, the next-door neighbor of South Vietnam. It was a direct response to the President's unilateral ordering of "incursions" into Cambodia in April 1970 to attack Vietcong bases there. Finally, in 1973, Congress passed the *War Powers Resolution*, an attempt to curb Presidential power over war that had grown beyond restraint since President Truman authorized American participation in the Korean Conflict in 1950. President Nixon vetoed the resolution, but Congress enacted it over his veto. The War Powers Resolution sets up a complex system of required reporting on American military involvement and voting by Congress to approve or reject such involvement; it has not successfully restrained later Presidents, however.

President Nixon's re-election in 1972 gave rise to what seemed at first a comic farce. Five employees of the Committee to Re-Elect the President (CREEP) were arrested in June 1972 during an attempted break-in at the Democratic National Committee headquarters at the Watergate apartment complex in Washington, D.C. The Watergate break-in had little effect on the November election, in which Nixon routed his Democratic opponent, Senator George McGovern of South Dakota, who had unsuccessfully pleaded with the news media to explore the Watergate break-in. When journalists from the *Washington Post* and other news organizations finally dug into the story, Watergate took on larger dimensions and a sinister cast.

In early 1973, the Senate appointed a select committee to investigate the unraveling scandal. Chaired by Democratic Senator Samuel J. Ervin, Jr., of North Carolina, the Watergate committee conducted nationally televised hearings throughout the spring and summer of 1973. It uncovered an extraordinary story of "dirty tricks" designed to eliminate all but the weakest Democratic candidates from the 1972 campaign and, even worse, a conspiracy to obstruct justice in the investigation of the Watergate break-in, which involved the FBI, the CIA, and even the highest levels of government.

President Nixon was forced by early revelations, even before Senator Ervin's committee convened, to accept the resignations of his closest aides, Chief of Staff H. R. Haldeman and Domestic Affairs Adviser John R. Ehrlichman, and of his Attorney General, Richard H. Kleindienst. But these resignations did not end the scandal or the investigations. The discovery that the President had tape-recorded White House conversations, including discussions of the attempt to stage a cover-up of the break-in, provoked the major controversies of the Watergate affair. The President's new Attorney General, Elliot Richardson, had appointed a special prosecutor, Harvard Law School professor Archibald Cox, to conduct an investigation of the case. When Cox insisted on subpoenaing the White House's tape recordings of critical meetings, the President directed the Attorney General to fire him. This demand led to the notorious "Saturday Night Massacre" in October 1973, which cost the two highest officials of the

Justice Department their jobs and astonished the nation. The Watergate inquiry took on new momentum. The President was forced to retreat from his harsh stand. A new special prosecutor carried on where Cox had left off. The burgeoning disclosures and discoveries of the various investigations into Watergate led to another series of televised Congressional hearings in the spring and summer of 1974.

The Constitution provides for a process of *impeachment* by which high officials, including the President of the United States, can be tried and removed from office for "Treason, Bribery, or other high Crimes and Misdemeanors." In the modern Congress, the House Judiciary Committee is the place where charges of impeachment are first brought. In July 1974, the committee, led by its chairman, Democratic Representative Peter J. Rodino of New Jersey, conducted formal hearings and debates on the question of impeaching the President of the United States. Not for over a century had an impeachment movement against a President gone this far. Rodino presided over the hearings with dignity and fairness; the members of the committee, Democrats and Republicans, opponents and defenders of the President, generally matched Rodino's high standard. On July 24, 1974, the Supreme Court ruled, eight to zero, against the President's attempts to resist the special prosecutor's subpoena for the White House tape recordings. Three days later, the committee voted, twenty-seven to eleven, to recommend articles of impeachment to the full House. The special prosecutor turned over further evidence to the House Judiciary Committee as he received it. Within a week, the eleven dissenters had changed their minds and agreed to support the first resolution, charging the President with obstruction of justice in the Watergate case. On August 8, 1974, Richard Nixon bowed to the inevitable and resigned from the Presidency.

The Watergate hearings conducted by the House and the Senate presented substantial evidence of Presidential wrong-

The House Judiciary Committee, under the chairmanship of Peter J. Rodino (Democrat–New Jersey), debated the impeachment of President Richard M. Nixon in July 1974. The committee voted to send three articles of impeachment to the full House of Representatives; these charges focused on President Nixon's abuses of power and obstruction of justice in the Watergate scandal. Nixon resigned on August 8, after making public damning evidence of his guilt but before the full House could vote on the issue of impeachment. Chairman Rodino is the white-haired man in the top row, just under the American flag.

doing before the American people. They were a valuable lesson in the ways that the Constitution and the system of government it authorizes are supposed to work. They also restored the dignity and credibility of Congress and diminished the previously unshakable authority of the Presidency.

In the fall of 1973, Vice President Spiro T. Agnew had resigned his office due to charges of alleged wrongdoing having nothing to do with Watergate. President Nixon had named and Congress had confirmed a replacement under the Twenty-Fifth Amendment to the Constitution, House Minority Leader Gerald R. Ford of Michigan. When Nixon resigned in August 1974, Vice President Ford became President. His pledge to the nation—"Our long national nightmare is over"—reassured the American people. At last, they hoped, politics would return to normal.

CHAPTER TWELVE

THE MODERN CONGRESS

Since the resignation of Richard Nixon, the federal government has continued to experience great stresses and strains, testing the durability of the system of government created by the Constitution. Those who hoped for a resumption of normal politics after Watergate were destined to be disappointed.

The aftereffects of Watergate included select committee investigations by both the House and the Senate of the conduct and abuses of power of American intelligence agencies. But Congress soon found itself challenged to live up to the higher ethical standards resulting from the Watergate scandal:

• Two powerful Democratic chairmen of House committees, Wilbur Mills of Arkansas (chairman of the Ways and Means Committee) and Wayne Hays of Ohio (chairman of the Administration Committee), were toppled from power after revelations of their scandalous private lives.

• The worst case was the FBI's so-called ABSCAM operation. Agents posing as Arab sheiks seeking favorable treatment from members of Congress on immigration matters in exchange for bribes managed to catch six Representatives and one Senator. All seven fell from power soon after the FBI unveiled ABSCAM; they faced criminal charges based on the operation.

• Finally, the House was forced to investigate itself concerning charges arising out of the "Koreagate" scandal, in which South Korean financier Tongsun Park allegedly had bribed several Representatives to vote favorably on aid for South Korea. The investigation ended inconclusively.

These and other scandals involving Congress undid much of the prestige that Congress had acquired for its handling of the Watergate scandal. In the meantime, President Ford had pardoned former President Nixon for his involvement in the Watergate affair. Ford suffered considerable political damage for this gesture. Taken together, these incidents injured the reputation of government and of politicians across the board.

Congress sought to improve its methods of doing business and its image by reforming its systems of assigning members to committees, by revamping the structure and number of committees, and by opening its proceedings to television coverage. The House and then the Senate permitted gavel-to-gavel coverage of their sessions.

Congress's relations with President Ford were not as stormy as they had been with President Nixon, but the two branches of government did not work comfortably together. Nor did conditions improve under Ford's successor, Democrat Jimmy Carter of Georgia. Carter had defeated his rivals for the 1976 Democratic Presidential nomination and then the Republican nominee, President Ford, by portraying himself as an outsider, not tainted by the "mess in Washington." But his status as an "outsider" prevented him from working well with Congress, and some of his advisers, the so-called "Georgia Mafia," openly disdained Congress. In response, the new Speaker of the House, Thomas P. "Tip" O'Neill of Massachusetts, sought to defend Congress and to guide the Carter Administration in the proper ways to deal with its sister institution. O'Neill was one of the more effective Speakers of the century, a master of the "old politics" who was uncomfortable with the impatient, scrappy practitioners of the "new politics" who thronged into the House in the late 1970s. O'Neill emulated Sam Rayburn's methods, favoring moderation and persuasion rather than arm-twisting and pressure. O'Neill's counterpart in the Senate was Democratic Majority Leader Robert C. Byrd of West Virginia, another traditional politician who respected the traditions and heritage of the Senate and tried to defend those traditions against younger colleagues of both parties.

President Carter managed to secure Senate ratification of a treaty restoring ultimate control over the Panama Canal to Panama. Its supporters hailed the treaty as a long-overdue redress of a great wrong the United States had committed against Panama; its opponents denounced it as a giveaway of a vital American possession. The President was not so fortunate in his attempts to ratify a strategic arms limitation treaty (SALT) he had negotiated with the Soviet Union. The SALT II treaty built on an earlier accord, the handiwork of President Nixon. But conservative Senators blocked the treaty, hoping for a favorable result in the 1980 Presidential election. They got their wish: President Carter was defeated for re-election by the Republican nominee, former Governor Ronald W. Reagan of California.

Reagan, at sixty-nine the oldest man ever elected to the Presidency, ran as an outsider, as Carter had, but did so far more effectively. He promised to reduce the size of the government, to cut federal spending, to cut taxes, to increase defense spending, and to balance the budget. He was so popular that, for the first time in a generation, the Republicans won control of the Senate.

Reagan's landslide gave him a remarkable political mandate—a mandate given a new lease on life by John W.

Hinckley's attempt to assassinate him two months after the inauguration. During his first term in office, the President rammed nearly all of his agenda through a reeling Congress. Only the House, led by Speaker O'Neill, put up resistance to "the Reagan Revolution." But the President's policies did not have the effect that he promised. The budget deficit did not go away; instead, it increased dramatically. The economic recovery caused by the tax cut did not produce the increased revenues that the President had hoped for. And his efforts to cut the federal budget ran into difficulty in both houses of Congress as Representatives and Senators alike balked at cutting popular "entitlement" programs such as Social Security.

The President asserted broad executive authority over foreign policy and defense issues. In October 1983, he ordered American forces into combat on the tiny Caribbean island of Grenada in the West Indies. The President claimed that American citizens (medical students attending a medical school on the island) were in danger from a Marxist coup. When angered members of Congress charged that the President had disregarded the War Powers Resolution of 1973, the President responded by expressing grave doubts about the constitutionality of the measure.

President Reagan easily won a second term in 1984, defeating Democratic nominee (and President Carter's Vice President) Walter F. Mondale. But his second term was more difficult and less successful than his first:

• The 1986 Congressional elections resulted in the return of a Democrat-controlled Senate determined to resist proposals by the Reagan Administration.

• An emboldened Congress overturned the President's vetoes of several key pieces of legislation. His most crushing defeat was Congress's 1988 override (73–24 in the Senate and 292–133 in the House) of the Civil Rights Restoration Act.

• The Senate rejected his nomination of Judge Robert H. Bork to the Supreme Court by the largest margin ever recorded for a vote against a Court nominee. His next choice, Judge Douglas H. Ginsburg, withdrew his name after allegations surfaced concerning his use of marijuana while he was a professor at Harvard Law School. Not until his third try did the President succeed. Judge Anthony Kennedy of California was unanimously confirmed by the Senate in early 1988.

• Finally, and most seriously, the President's long campaign to support the anti-Communist Nicaraguan rebels, the *contras*, against the Marxist Sandinista government of that country caused him his most serious problems. Congress refused to fund the *contras* and passed a measure, known as the Boland Amendment, forbidding the government to aid the *contras* with federal funds. Within President Reagan's National Security Council, an operation developed to raise funds for the *contras* from other sources, including arms deals with the hostile nation of Iran. When this scandal broke in late 1986, several congressional committees leaped into the fray. The scattered and disorganized investigations continued into early 1987, when the leadership of Congress agreed to appoint two select committees to hold joint hearings on the matter. The Iran-*contra* investigation continued through the summer and fall of 1987, coinciding with the Bork confirmation controversy and the two-hundredth anniversary of the Constitution. Those hoping for an investigation of the quality of the Watergate hearings of the 1970s were disappointed. (The Iran-*contra* matter is still unresolved at this writing.)

Speaker O'Neill retired in 1987 and was succeeded by the House Majority Leader, Democrat Jim Wright of Texas. Wright's Speakership was fiercely attacked by Republicans in the House, who charged that the Speaker's open partisanship was making a mockery of the rules and traditions of the House. Some observers suggested that the nearly thirty years of unbroken Democratic control of the House caused some leading Democrats to treat the Republican minority as an inconvenience rather than as a group of colleagues with differing political views.

The Senate's long traditions of collegiality (relations of mutual respect among colleagues) and institutional pride have ensured that it is largely free of the partisan bitterness plaguing the modern House of Representatives. But the Senate has problems of its own. In April 1988, Republican Daniel Evans of Washington published an important article in *The New York Times Magazine* entitled "Why I'm Quitting the Senate." Senator Evans spelled out some of the reasons for his frustration with what he described as "a legislative body that [has] lost its focus and [is] in danger of losing its soul": manipulation of Senate rules to force needless votes; excessive use of filibusters or the threats of filibusters; the impossibility of any Senator having a personal or family life due to the burdens of committee assignments, pointless roll calls, and the pressures of constituents; the lack of attention to formal debate; Senators' tendencies to accept or seek more committee and subcommittee assignments than they can reasonably handle; and a general erosion of respect for the values of the Senate as an institution. Senator Evans described his efforts, with colleagues of both parties, to conduct informal "Quality of Life" discussions to improve life in the Senate. Still, he noted, "The Senate campaign of 1988 . . . may well be remembered . . . for those who chose not to run. Seldom have so many Senators in midcareer chosen to call it quits."

INTO THE THIRD CENTURY

As the form of government authorized by the Constitution completed its first two hundred years, several proposals have circulated for restructuring the government of the United States.

Some call for the adoption of a *parliamentary* system of government, like that of Great Britain or Canada. Under this system, the national legislature would be the central institution of government. Political parties would compete to win a majority of seats in the national legislature, and the leaders of the majority party would become the Prime Minister and other Ministers of the government. If the government is put to the test in the legislature—what is called a *vote of confidence*—and loses, the leaders then resign their executive offices, and a new election is held. A separately elected executive, such as a President, would serve the same function as the monarch does in Great Britain: to perform ceremonial tasks and responsibilities, to accept the resignation of a toppled Prime Minister, and to call upon the leader of the victorious party in a parliamentary election to form a new administration. This proposal is popular with many political scientists who favor ways to make the political parties stronger in our system of government. Most Americans, however, are not ready for such a sweeping measure.

Less extreme proposals include amendments to:

• Permit former Presidents and Cabinet members to sit as nonvoting Senators and to take part in debate so that the nation can still profit from their knowledge and experience;

• Permit Cabinet members to sit in either the House or the Senate so that they are able and required to engage with Congress in debate of Administration policy;

• Extend the term of Representatives from two to four years and schedule House elections to coincide with Presidential elections, strengthening the parties in the constitutional system.

None of these three proposals has won significant support outside the scholarly community so far.

Of the three branches of government created by the Constitution, Congress has the lowest reputation and the most uncertain future. Although buffeted by passionate criticism of some of its decisions, the Supreme Court enjoys the respect of most Americans. And, despite charges growing out of the Iran-*contra* affair, the Presidency has managed to regain much of the prestige it lost as a result of the Watergate scandals. Congress, on the other hand, still suffers from public scorn— when, indeed, the public consents to think about Congress at all.

What are the causes of the low public opinion of Congress? As we suggested at the beginning of this book, the reason in part may be the public's growing impatience with and lack of understanding of politics—the bargaining and horse-trading and compromising out of which public policies and legislation emerge. Of the three branches of our government, Congress is the most clearly and unavoidably political. The Supreme Court is a legal institution; most people do not think of it as political. And it has long been a favorite tactic of Presidents to claim that they are speaking for the general interest, the common good, and not being political. Congress has no choice in the matter.

Congress could recover its lost authority—if the American people learn once again to accept that the Constitution divides the powers and responsibilities of government among three branches: the legislative, the executive, and the judiciary. Congress is a key part of that delicately balanced structure.

Congress does not have a monopoly on the shaping of government policy; that became clear in the first decade of its existence. But Congress is the only institution of our government where representatives of different states, different sections of the country, different economic and cultural and ethnic and racial interests can come together and discuss what policies would be best for the nation as a whole. Congress is the only part of our government that permits—even demands—wide-ranging debate over how government policies are to be framed and how they are to be carried out.

Many people express impatience with the slowness of Congress, with its members' obsession with politics and their inability to get things done. But public policy is not made instantly. It is not like fast food or television commercials, which do their job quickly and leave no trace behind. Public policy is made slowly, often with great care. The compromises and uncertainties of what Congress does are necessary, in part, to make certain that it does its job well.

Today *politics* is a dirty word for most Americans. But politics is the only successful way that human beings have found to make sure that government performs its role without endangering the rights of individuals. It may be slow, it may be boring, it may sometimes even be ugly or depressing—but politics is central to the way that we govern ourselves.

Perhaps the only way that Congress will become an institution as deserving of respect as the Presidency and the Supreme Court is for the American people to rediscover the need for—and the virtues of—politics.

FOR FURTHER READING

(An asterisk indicates that a paperback edition is available.)

The best introduction to the Constitution's principles and history is John Sexton and Nat Brandt, *How Free Are We? What the Constitution Says We Can and Cannot Do* (New York: M. Evans, 1986)*; a more unconventional and very popular treatment is Jerome Agel and Mort Gerberg, *The U.S. Constitution for Everyone* (New York: Perigee/Putnam, 1987)*. An excellent short general history of the United States is Allan Nevins and Henry Steele Commager, *A Pocket History of the United States*, 7th ed. (New York: Pocket Books, 1987)*. The best single-volume constitutional history of the United States is Alfred H. Kelly, Winfred A. Harbison, and Herman Belz, *The American Constitution: Its Origins and Development*, 6th ed. (New York: Norton, 1983). The best study of the Federal Convention of 1787 is Clinton L. Rossiter, *1787: The Grand Convention* (New York: Norton, 1987)*. Richard B. Bernstein with Kym S. Rice, *Are We to Be a Nation? The Making of the Constitution* (Cambridge, Mass.: Harvard University Press, 1987)*, presents an overview of the era of the American Revolution based on the latest scholarship.

Other than highly technical political science monographs, very few studies of Congress exist. The handful of good general books includes Alvin M. Josephy, Jr., *On the Hill* (New York: Simon & Schuster, 1979); Richard A. Baker, *The Senate of the United States: A Bicentennial History* (Malabar, Fla.: Robert E. Krieger, 1988)*; and James Currie, *The U.S. House of Representatives: A Bicentennial History* (Malabar, Fla.: Robert E. Krieger, 1988)*.

INDEX